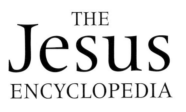

THE
Jesus
ENCYCLOPEDIA

THE
Jesus
ENCYCLOPEDIA

LOIS ROCK

Text by Lois Rock
Copyright © 2005 Lion Hudson plc
Illustrations © 2005 Peter Dennis
(unless otherwise stated opposite)

North American edition published by Tommy Nelson®,
a Division of Thomas Nelson, Inc.

Original edition published in English under the title
The Jesus Encyclopedia by Lion Hudson plc, Oxford, England.
Copyright © 2005 Lion Hudson plc.

Scripture quotations are from the Good News Bible
published by The Bible Societies/HarperCollins Publishers,
copyright © 1966, 1971, 1976, 1992 American Bible Society.

Typeset in 12/15 Latin 725 BT

ISBN: 1400305276

Printed in Singapore

05 06 07 08 09 TWP 5 4 3 2 1

Picture Acknowledgments

t=top, b=bottom, c=centre, l=left, r=right

David Alexander: pp. 11t/c (British Museum), 16t/c/b, 17tr/cr, 30l, 31l,
32l, 33t, 36r, 48, 55r, 69b, 77b, 81b, 83tr, 94l, 98t, 101t, 114.
Jon Arnold Images: p. 101b.
Bodleian Library, University of Oxford: pp. 8tr/c/br, 9r (ms. auct. t. inf. 1.
10, folios 80v, 23v, 118v, 178v).
The British Library: p. 9l.
British Museum: pp. 10, 72t.
Lion Hudson: pp. 76r; 14r, 17br, 31l, 32l, 34l, 45br, 46r, 51tl, 68br, 70t,
73b, 74b, 83l, 84t, 95r, 96l, 112b/David Townsend; 19b, 25b, 27tr, 29t,
31r, 35r, 45tl, 56 (all), 59br, 62l, 63c/b, 64, 69r, 76t, 87tl/br, 101c,
106l/John Williams.
Jerry Irwin: p. 57r. Copyright © Jerry Irwin. Used by permission of
Good Books (www.goodbks.com). All rights reserved.
John Rylands University Library of Manchester: p. 8tl.
Rex Nicholls: pp. 7bc, 11br, 12l, 13r, 19t, 20l, 36l, 39t, 46bl, 53, 58b, 67t,
71b, 81t/c, 82l, 83br, 89t, 93b, 102.
Photo Oikoumene/World Council of Churches: pp. 85cr/br, 120–21 (all).
Zev Radovan, Jerusalem: p. 46br.
Lois Rock: pp. 54l, 66t, 74t, 77tr, 90l, 98bl, 99t.
Nick Rous: p. 60.
Derek West: maps on pp. 7t, 17, 68bl, 112t, 115.

Picture research below courtesy of Zooid Pictures Limited.

Alamy: p. 79r/Jeremy Hoare.
AKG - Images: pp. 6 and 87tr/Pirozzi, 24b, 27b/Cameraphoto, 51tr and
88/Erich Lessing, 95l, 100t, 113t, 117.
Art Directors & Trip Photo Library: p. 108l/David Butcher.
Bridgeman Art Library: pp. 65b, 76l.
British Museum: p. 63tr/Zooid Pictures.
Corbis UK Ltd: pp. 23b/Archivo Iconografico, S.A., 33b/Alain
Nogues/Sygma, 43/Hans Georg Roth, 45tr/Reza Sygma, 61cr/Hanan
Isachar, 75b/Araldo de Luca, 91/Bettmann, 92/Richard T. Nowitz,
97t/John Garrett, 107r/Dave Bartruff, 111t/The Barnes Foundation,
Merion Station, Pennsylvania, 120l/Joel Sartore.
Edifice: p. 7r.
PA Photos: p. 89b/Johnny Green.
Rex Features: p. 41b/Paul Felix.
Zev Radovan, Jerusalem: pp. 14l, 38l, 59bc.

Contents

1  Introducing Jesus

Look It Up

Jesus' name and family line:
Matthew 1, Luke 1–2

Roman rulers in Jesus' day:
Matthew 2, 14, 27, Mark 6, 15, Luke 1, 2, 3, 9, 23, John 18, 19

Christry

Christ

The title "Christ" that is often linked with Jesus comes from a Greek word. When news of Jesus first spread out through the Roman empire from the land where he had lived, Greek was the language commonly used by many different nations. However, the word *Christ* is a translation of a Hebrew word found in the Scriptures of Jesus' people. That word is *messiah,* and Christians also say that Jesus is the Messiah.

One of the earliest pictures of Jesus, painted a little over three hundred years after he lived.

Jesus is the central figure of one of the world's great religions: Christianity. Followers of Jesus are called Christians.

The words *Christianity* and *Christian* come from the word *Christ,* the title most commonly linked with the name of Jesus: "Jesus Christ." This title means "anointed one," and anointing is a ceremony of king making. Jesus' followers believe that Jesus is God's king.

Jesus lived on earth around two thousand years ago. He belonged to a people who thought of themselves as God's chosen people. In the past, they had been known as the people of Israel, but by the time of Jesus they were often known as the Jews. Jesus lived in the land where his people had made their home for hundreds of years—a land on the eastern shore of the Mediterranean Sea. In the time of Jesus, it was part of the Roman empire.

This picture shows local people hurrying away from a troop of soldiers marching through Galilee. Whatever the Roman soldiers demanded, the people had to obey. For example, a soldier could force a passer-by to carry his heavy pack for a mile or more.

In the time of Jesus the Roman empire included many lands around the Mediterranean Sea. The emperor ruled from the capital city of Rome. Lesser officials were put in charge of smaller regions. At the time Jesus was born, a half-Jewish man named Herod was king in Jerusalem on behalf of the Romans. Years later, when Jesus died, the Roman governor Pontius Pilate was in charge.

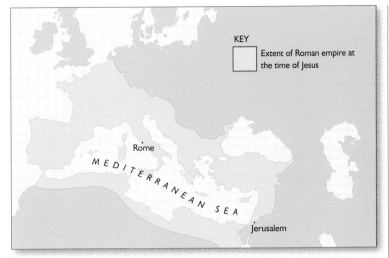

KEY

Extent of Roman empire at the time of Jesus

Rome

MEDITERRANEAN SEA

Jerusalem

Jesus was never crowned a king. While he was alive, some of his followers hoped that he might try to seize power from those who ruled the land, but Jesus was not a fighting man. He was famous in his own day as a teacher and for preaching about God in the towns and villages around his home in the region of Galilee and, further away, in his people's city of Jerusalem.

His teaching was popular with some, especially the poor and the outcasts; however, the religious leaders were often puzzled by what he said, and many of them feared that his teaching was wrong and that his popularity was becoming a danger. In the end, they became so angry they plotted to have him put to death.

However, his followers continued to spread his teaching. What they said about Jesus sparked a new movement, first among the Jews, then among the non-Jews, the Gentiles.

This movement was the beginning of Christianity. It is a faith that has shaped a good deal of the history of the past two thousand years; it is a faith that has spread around the world.

The Roman emperor, Augustus Caesar, stands wearing his military breastplate. He reigned during the first half of Jesus' life.

The Western calendar

The Christian faith that Jesus inspired has been a major influence in history. For much of the first fifteen centuries it was particularly important in European countries—so important that the Western calendar that was developed there still counts the years from his birth.

You will sometimes see the letters "AD" before the number of the year in the Western calendar. The letters stand for the Latin words anno Domini, meaning, "in the year of the Lord"—referring to Jesus Christ. If you see the letters "BC" after the number of a year it indicates that the year is "before Christ."

Other faiths and cultures have their own calendars, but the Western calendar is widely used around the world. It has therefore become quite usual to use the letters "CE" instead of AD and "BCE" instead of BC. They stand for Common Era and Before the Common Era respectively.

The letters "AD" in front of a year are a clear reminder of the link between Christianity and the Western calendar. This inscription is on a chapel in Wales.

2 ✾ How Do We Know About Jesus?

Look It Up

How do we know about Jesus?
Luke 1, John 20, 21

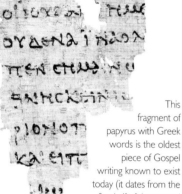

This fragment of papyrus with Greek words is the oldest piece of Gospel writing known to exist today (it dates from the first half of the second century CE). It shows verses from the Gospel of John.

Gospels and evangelists

The books of Matthew, Mark, Luke, and John are called the Gospels. Today they are part of the Christian Bible. They are the first four books of the section that Christians call the New Testament.

The word *gospel* comes from old English words meaning "a good tale," "good news." The Greek word for good news has given rise to another word for gospel, *evangel*. This word is rarely used, but the Gospel writers are often called the evangelists.

News about Jesus and his message first began to spread because the things he said and did left people amazed. They simply couldn't stop talking about it. After Jesus left the world, his followers went out telling people they met in the streets and in the marketplaces and anywhere that people met together. As time went by, Jesus' followers began to write down some of the things they knew, and some of these writings still exist. Christians consider the accounts of Jesus' life to be the most important of these.

Mark

People believe that one of Jesus' followers may have begun to write down stories very soon after his death. The earliest account that still exists today is called Mark. Ancient traditions say that the writer was John Mark, who traveled with a group of followers to many countries around the Roman empire spreading the message.

Mark.

Matthew and Luke

Matthew.

Two other existing accounts are called Matthew and Luke. The writers of these accounts have many of the same stories that are found in Mark—sometimes in the same words. Many people believe that both writers used Mark's account to help them.

Matthew and Luke also have some extra stories that are very similar. Scholars think they may have used another collection of stories, which they call "Q," as a source for their writing.

Matthew and Luke each have some stories that are only found in their account. Indeed, Luke went on to write a second book, about what Jesus' followers did after his death. It is called The Acts of the Apostles.

Luke.

8

John

There is one more key account, and it is quite different from the other three. This is the account of John. An ancient tradition says that this was the same John who was a disciple of Jesus and knew him for the three years he spent teaching and preaching.

John dictating his Gospel.

The Lindisfarne Gospels are one of the great treasures of the Christian faith. This copy of the Vulgate with ornate lettering and decorations was made between 715 and 720 by monks who lived on the island of Lindisfarne, off the northeast coast of England.

✠ Good news for all people

From the time that Christians first gathered their Scriptures together, the Gospels have been held in the highest esteem.

Originally written in Greek, the Gospels, along with other Bible books, were soon translated into other languages. Christians in different countries wanted to hear the stories of Jesus for themselves.

One of the earliest translations was into Coptic, a form of ancient Egyptian. The Coptic Bible is still used in the Coptic churches of northwest Africa.

Another was into Syriac. This language was a type of Aramaic, the language Jesus probably spoke. The Syriac translation, the Peshitta, is still used by Christians in Syria, Iran, and India. It is also used by one of the Christian groups who take care of the Church of the Holy Sepulchre in Jerusalem, and many Christians from all over the world gather to hear it read aloud. It gives them a chance to hear the words of Jesus in a form similar to the actual words he would have used.

When Christianity became the official religion of the Roman empire in 312, it became increasingly important to have one reliable translation of the Bible in Latin. A monk named Jerome undertook the work in 384. His translation, known as the Vulgate, became the most important version of the Bible in the Western churches for the next thousand years. Around the fifth and sixth centuries, another translation was made into Old Slavonic, and this became the official Bible of the Russian Orthodox church in the East.

In the Middle Ages, Christian monks in Europe showed how much they treasured the Bible by producing richly decorated copies—usually of the Vulgate. Writing the whole Bible out by hand was a long job, and sometimes they chose to make copies of the Gospels only.

To this day, Christians who have taken their faith to different countries around the world and want to translate the Bible into local languages often begin with the Gospels. Printed together, they make a small book that is quite inexpensive to make—and can be sold very cheaply or given away.

Why write about Jesus?

Jesus' followers had several reasons for writing down what they knew about him:

• The people who had actually known Jesus were getting old: it was important that their stories would not be forgotten.
• The message was spreading further and further: writings were easy to take to new groups of Christians so they could learn more about their new faith.
• Writings could also be read in secret. In the early days, it was against the law to be a Christian, so this was a great advantage.

Jesus in history

There are other early writings that talk about Jesus. With the New Testament writings, they amount to a lot of evidence that Jesus actually lived, had many followers, and was put to death by order of the local Roman governor, Pontius Pilate. A Jewish history written by someone called Flavius Josephus not long after Jesus' life on earth says this:

Now there was about this time Jesus, a wise man, for he was a doer of wonders. He drew many after him. When Pilate, at the suggestion of the principal men among us, had condemned him to the cross, those that loved him at the first did not forsake him, and the tribe of Christians, so named from him, are not extinct at this day.

Antiquities 18:63–64

3  The Jewish People

The Scriptures

The Jewish Scriptures told of the great agreements, or covenants, God made with the Jewish people, including those with Abraham and Moses. Another word that means the same as agreement, or covenant, is testament. Christians refer to the Jewish Scriptures as the Old Testament. These are the first part of the Christian Bible.

Christians believe that, by his death, Jesus created a new agreement between God and people. They call the collection of writings that tell of Jesus and his followers the New Testament. This is the second part of the Christian Bible.

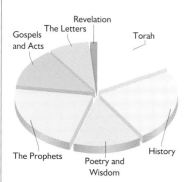

This chart shows the proportion of different types of literature in the Bible. The Gospels, Acts, Letters, and Revelation belong to the New Testament. The other types belong to the Old Testament.

Jesus' own people were the Jews. The ancient writings of the Jews reveal their growing trust in their God to take care of them.

The people of Israel

As a people, the Jews traced their beginnings to someone called Abraham. The stories about him are set in the Bronze Age, possibly as much as two thousand years before Jesus. The writings said that God had made an agreement with Abraham: God was going to give him a land where his descendants would become a great people. His people must respect God, and God would look after them and, through them, bring a blessing to all the world. This agreement was handed down to Abraham's descendants, including his grandson, Jacob, renamed Israel.

This ancient tomb painting from Egypt shows a clan of Semitic traders—people from the same ethnic group as Abraham and his descendants. The people in the Bible stories of this period probably had these styles of brightly patterned clothing.

The Law of Moses

Hundreds of years passed. By that time, the people of Israel had become slaves in Egypt. God chose someone to rescue them: Moses led them to freedom in their old land. Through Moses, God gave the people laws to live by. The early stories of the people of Israel and the Law of Moses are found in five books known collectively as the Torah.

Kings

In the new land the people struggled to stay free of their enemies. In the end, God helped them choose kings to lead them to freedom. The first two—Saul and David—set the country free. The third, Solomon, made it powerful and rich. He built the first Temple in the city of Jerusalem, which David had captured.

The history books of the Old Testament tell the story of these kings and the ones who came after them. It was from the time of Solomon that books of poetry and wisdom were written, including the book of Psalms, which were used in Temple worship.

This Assyrian carving shows the defeat of the city of Lachish—one of the cities in the southern kingdom of Judah—in 701 BCE. The Israelites did not make pictures of themselves, as they believed God's laws forbade it, so this is one of very few pictures of a Bible event.

Prophets

After Solomon's reign, the kingdom split into north and south. In the north, the people did not stay faithful to God, in spite of warnings from the prophets. After a few centuries they were destroyed by the Assyrians.

In the south, around Jerusalem, the people were more faithful. They, too, had prophets to help them and survived the Assyrian wars. Later, however, they were defeated by the Babylonians.

In the years when the Assyrians threatened the people of Israel, a king named Jehu brought rich gifts to the emperor Shalmaneser. This carving shows Jehu bowing low.

The Temple was destroyed, and many of the people were resettled in Babylon. The books of the prophets provide a commentary on these events.

Hope for a king

The prophets also spoke words of hope: one day, they believed, God would send a new king—a messiah, like David—to rescue them.

When the Babylonians were defeated by the Persians, the Jews were allowed home and built a new Temple. They began to study their Scriptures with more zeal than ever. When they were conquered by the Greeks and then the Romans, their hope for a messiah grew stronger.

Who is God?

Christians and Jews believe in the same God, the one spoken of in the Old Testament and by Jesus himself—who was, of course, a Jew.

Here are some words from Psalms—the hymnbook of the Old Testament—that talk about God, the one they believed had made heaven and earth and was the one true God.

To you alone, O Lord, to you alone,
and not to us, must glory be given
because of your constant love and
faithfulness. . . .
Trust in the Lord, you people of Israel.
He helps you and protects you. . . .
Trust in the Lord, all you that
worship him.
He helps you and protects you.
The Lord remembers us and will
bless us;
he will bless the people of Israel
and all the priests of God.
He will bless everyone who
honors him,
the great and the small alike. . . .
May you be blessed by the Lord,
who made heaven and earth!

Psalms 115:1, 9, 11–13, 15

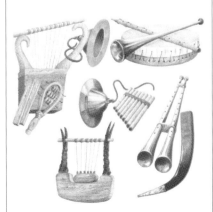

Instruments such as these were used to accompany the singing of psalms in Temple worship. The style of music was often noisy and exuberant.

4 The Jewish Faith in Jesus' Day

Look It Up

The Temple:
*Exodus 25–27, 30, 33, 35–40,
1 Kings 5–8, 2 Kings 25*

Passover:
*Exodus 12, Leviticus 23, Numbers 28,
Deuteronomy 16*

The story of the Temple

The design of the Temple followed instructions that God had given Moses. As the people traveled to the land where they were going to make their home, God had told them to make a place of worship called the tabernacle. It was an elaborate tent that could be moved from place to place.

In the time of Jesus, the faith of the Jews was well organized and carefully guarded by its leaders.

The Temple

The worship of God was centered on ceremonies in the Temple in Jerusalem. King Solomon had used the same design when he built the first Temple in Jerusalem. That Temple was destroyed when the armies of Babylon invaded, but when the Jewish people were given permission to return to their city, they built another one. Times had been hard, and everyone lamented that the second Temple was not nearly as grand as the first.

Around the time of Jesus, a local king saw his chance. Herod was not a religious man—in fact he was power hungry and very cruel—but he knew that he could make himself look good by organizing the building of a splendid new Temple.

Temple worship

At the Temple, priests were in charge of the religious ceremonies. Every day they kept the lamps in the inner part of the Temple alight and burned sweet-smelling incense. Other officials, called Levites, helped with the administration of the Temple. This involved making sure that pilgrims could buy the animals they needed to offer for sacrifice and change their local money into the special coins needed to pay the Temple tax.

Holy Place
Priests were allowed into the sanctuary as far as the Holy Place in this building. Beyond, screened by a richly woven curtain, was the Holy of Holies. This dark room was reserved for the ark of the covenant—the box containing God's laws—even though the one made for Solomon's Temple had been lost in the wars hundreds of years earlier.

Court of Israel
Only Jewish men were allowed in the Court of Israel. Animal sacrifices to God were burned on a huge altar here.

Court of the women
Both Jewish men and Jewish women could enter the court of the women—but women were allowed no further.

Court of the Gentiles
The main Temple building shown here stood in a much larger courtyard called the Court of the Gentiles. Non-Jews were only allowed as far as this courtyard, where traders and moneychangers ran their stalls.

A Passover meal in the time of Jesus included roast lamb and bread without yeast, as on the first Passover night.

Passover

Passover was the greatest festival in the Jewish year. It remembered the night God had enabled Moses to lead the people out of Egypt and to freedom. The Temple priests organized special ceremonies to celebrate the event.

On that first Passover, God had told the people of Israel to prepare a special meal and mark their houses with the blood of a lamb. Then the angel of death passed over their houses, but in the unmarked houses of the Egyptians, every firstborn died. In their grief and fear, the Egyptians let the Israelites go.

The dream of every devout Jew was to be in Jerusalem for Passover.

5 More About the Jewish Faith

Look It Up

Jesus in the synagogues:
Matthew 4, 9, 12, 13, Mark 1, 3, 6,
Luke 4, 6, 13, John 6

An ancient fragment of scripture, written in Hebrew.

Keeping the faith

From the time of the exile onwards, the Jewish faith was more and more linked to knowing and understanding the collection of scriptures that had been gathered. So began the practice of copying the writings with great attention to detail and accuracy.

The picture above shows part of the Isaiah scroll found at Qumran by the Dead Sea. It dates from around 100 bce. The words are virtually identical to those found in modern copies of the scriptures because the scribes took such care with what they believed was the word of God.

In the time of Jesus, the Jews regularly met in their communities to worship God and to learn more about how to live as God's people.

Synagogue and Scripture

Centuries before the time of Jesus, when the Babylonians had destroyed the Temple and taken the people into exile, a new way of worshiping had begun. The Jewish people took to meeting together on their weekly day of rest, the Sabbath.

At the same time, well-educated scribes set about collecting and organizing the people's Scriptures—both the oldest writings that told of Moses and their history, and newer writings from wise men, poets, and the followers of the prophets.

In their meeting places, the synagogues, the Scriptures were read aloud. All Jewish men were supposed to take part in the actual reading, and teachers, called rabbis, helped explain the meaning to the people.

By the time of Jesus, even small communities had their own synagogue buildings, with rabbis and other officials.

The ruins in this photo show the remains of a first-century building in Gamla, near Galilee. Experts agree the building was probably a synagogue that was destroyed not long after the time of Jesus, when the Romans defeated a Jewish rebellion. It is quite possible that Jesus visited the synagogue and preached here.

A Sabbath meeting

The synagogue buildings were designed as places for people to meet, but they were full of reminders of the Temple. There, the innermost room—the Holy of Holies—had been screened by a curtain. Within was the ark of the covenant, and in the ark, a copy of the laws on which the covenant was based. In the synagogue, there was also an area screened by a curtain. Beyond was a cupboard—the "ark"— in which the scrolls of the law were kept. However, those scrolls were not regarded as untouchably holy. Instead, they were meant to be read and understood.

During the week, boys were able to go to a school at the synagogue where the rabbi taught them to read the Scriptures.

Ark
The cupboard where the scrolls containing the Scriptures were kept.

Men took turns reading the Scripture. A teacher—a rabbi—would help explain them.

Lampstand
The seven-branched lampstand, the *menorah*, was based on the instructions for a lampstand in the first tabernacle.

It was the custom for men and women to sit on opposite sides of the building.

This cutaway picture is based on the evidence found at two ancient synagogue sites—one at Gamla (opposite) and another at King Herod's fortress at Masada.

Religious groups

There were two important religious groups in the time of Jesus.

The Sadducees were mainly wealthy families and priests. They took the Law of Moses as it stood and were not expecting any new revelations from God. They were the most powerful group in the religious council in Jerusalem. This council was called the Sanhedrin.

The Pharisees included many scribes, who worked to preserve the Scriptures. They wanted to explain the old laws by working out in detail what was the right thing to do for everything that might happen in everyday life. They also studied the writings of the prophets. They believed that the Scriptures contained God's promise to send a king to restore the nation—a messiah. Many local rabbis were Pharisees.

6 Where Jesus Lived

The River Jordan rises in the marshy area north of Galilee.

The city of Jerusalem stands on a hilltop. It was the ancient city of the Jewish people, a natural fortress captured by their great king, David, hundreds of years earlier. In Jesus' day anyone looking towards the city from the Mount of Olives (where this picture was taken) would have seen the temple in the place where you now see a gold-domed mosque.

The land where Jesus lived borders the Mediterranean. Hills rise up from the strip of low land by the coast. Further east, the River Jordan flows through a deep valley. It rises among marshes in the north and flows through a lake called Galilee to the Dead Sea.

A view of Lake Galilee, also known as the Sea of Tiberias.

The southern part of the Jordan Valley and the area around the Dead Sea is noticeably hot and dry. Although the town of Jericho is built on a natural oasis, most of this region in Jesus' day was wilderness: the vegetation consisted of sparse pasture and thorny plants that could survive the dry conditions. Wild animals such as wolves and jackals lurked among the caves and crevasses.

In Galilee

Jesus grew up in Nazareth, among the hills of Galilee. Here, farmers grew barley, olives, and grapes. Shepherds grazed their flocks on the pastureland. Jesus' teaching often mentioned this rural setting.

When Jesus became a teacher, he spent much of his time in the

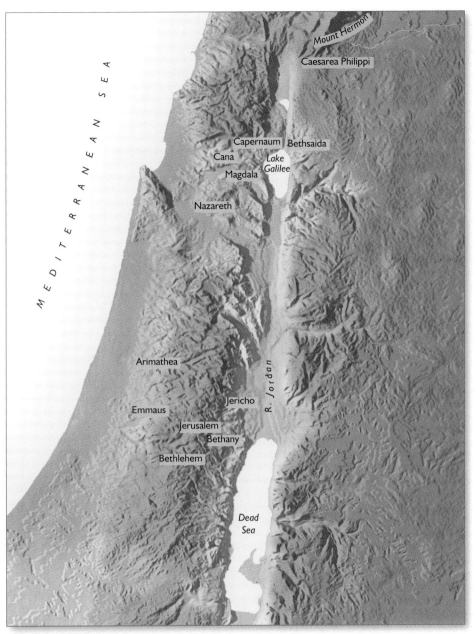

This map shows some of the most important places named in the accounts of Jesus' life. The shading also gives an idea of where there are hills and plains.

Bethlehem was a hilltop town surrounded by farmland. It was home to a shepherd boy named David before he became the nation's most famous king.

Away from the coast and the hills were dry areas of wild country—lonely places where wild animals and bandits roamed.

The Dead Sea is the lowest place on earth. It is a lake, and the water that flows into it can only escape by evaporation into the clouds, leaving behind any minerals and salts. As a result, the Dead Sea is now so salty that almost nothing can live in it.

towns and villages around Lake Galilee. Four of Jesus' closest friends were fishermen.

Around Jerusalem

The most important city was Jerusalem. All around was farmland: the hill opposite Jerusalem's Temple Mount was covered with olive groves and was called the Mount of Olives. Nearby Bethlehem was set among fertile hills where crops were grown: *Bethlehem* means "house of bread." It is famous as the place where Jesus was born.

7   Announcing Jesus: Mark's Account

Look It Up

The birth of John:
Luke 1

Announcing Jesus:
Mark 1, also Matthew 3, Luke 3, John 1

John's message:
Luke 3

The birth of John

Luke tells this story about the person known in the Christian faith as John the Baptist.

A couple had no children, and were now too old. The man, Zechariah, worked as a priest. One day, when he was in the Temple, an angel told him that his wife, Elizabeth, would have a son, John, who would be a prophet. Zechariah found this too hard to believe. The angel said that, as a sign, Zechariah would not be able to speak till the child was born.

Everything happened as the angel said. When it was time to name the newborn child, Zechariah wrote, "His name is John." At once he could speak and said:

"You, my child, will be called a
* prophet of the Most High God.*
You will go ahead of the Lord
* to prepare his road for him,*
to tell his people that they will be
* saved by having their sins*
forgiven."
Luke 1:76–77

Luke says that Elizabeth was the cousin of Jesus' mother, Mary.

The crowds believed that John was a prophet—he even dressed like a prophet from days past.

Any account of a person's life needs an introduction. All four Gospels introduce the life of Jesus in a special way. Mark's account—the shortest and almost certainly the first to be written—gets straight to the point.

He begins by declaring that Jesus is indeed the Christ, the Messiah the prophets spoke about:

This is the Good News about Jesus Christ, the Son of God. It began as the prophet Isaiah had written:
* "God said, 'I will send my messenger ahead of you*
*   to open the way for you.'*
* Someone is shouting in the desert,*
*   'Get the road ready for the Lord;*
*   make a straight path for him to travel!'"*
Mark 1:1–3

Mark then goes on to outline the work of that messenger. His name was John, and he lived like a prophet of old. He wore rough clothes made of camel's hair tied with a leather belt, and he lived in the desert where he fed himself on the food that he could find—locusts and wild honey. He preached to the crowds who came to listen to him: "Turn away from your sins and be baptized, and God will forgive your sins."

John baptized anyone who wanted to turn their lives around so they would be ready for God's Messiah. He dipped them in the River Jordan as a sign of being washed clean, a sign of saying goodbye to one way of life and rising to a fresh start. John became known as "John the Baptist."

One day, Jesus joined the crowds who had come to listen to John and to be baptized. During their meeting, something special happened. Mark says this:

As soon as Jesus came up out of the water, he saw heaven opening and the Spirit coming down on him like a dove. And a voice came from heaven, "You are my own dear Son. I am pleased with you."

Mark 1:10–11

This map shows the Jordan valley from Galilee in the north to the Dead Sea. It was here that John the Baptist preached and baptized. One Gospel reference says the people came to see him at Aenon.

John's message

All four accounts of Jesus' life mention John. Here is what Luke tells us about his teaching:

The people asked him, "What are we to do, then?"

He answered, "Whoever has two shirts must give one to the man who has none, and whoever has food must share it."

Some tax collectors came to be baptized, and they asked him, "Teacher, what are we to do?"

"Don't collect more than is legal," he told them.

Some soldiers also asked him, "What about us? What are we to do?"

He said to them, "Don't take money from anyone by force or accuse anyone falsely. Be content with your pay."

Luke 3:10–14

✚ Advent

Some Christian churches choose the four Sundays before Christmas as a special time to look forward to the birth of Jesus and to remember the important prophets and messengers who also looked forward to Jesus' coming. This period of time is called Advent, from a Latin word meaning "coming."

A special theme is set for each Sunday: the first is God's people, who looked forward to Jesus' coming; the second is the Old Testament prophets, who foretold his birth; the third is John the Baptist; and the fourth is Mary, the mother of Jesus.

One Advent tradition is to make an Advent wreath with four candles set around in the ring and a tall white candle in the center. The four candles are lit in turn on each of the four Sundays in Advent. On Christmas Day all four candles and the tall central candle are lit to celebrate the birth of Jesus, "the light of the world."

8 Announcing Jesus: John's Account

Look It Up

The Holy Spirit:
Matthew 4, Mark 1, Luke 3, John 1

Announcing Jesus:
John 1

The death of John the Baptist:
Matthew 14, Mark 6, Luke 9

✝ The Holy Spirit

In the story of Jesus' baptism, God's Holy Spirit settles on him in the form of a dove. As a result, this bird has become a symbol of the Holy Spirit.

The Old Testament story of Noah's ark also mentions a dove as one of the birds rescued from the flood. When the rain stopped, Noah sent the dove to search for land. It brought back an olive leaf in its beak, clear proof that the floodwaters had gone down and that God had kept everyone on the ark safe.

The symbolism of the dove in the two stories is often put together—a dove with an olive leaf in its beak becomes the symbol of God's Holy Spirit that both enables people to live in the right way and also protects them from danger.

The writer of the Gospel of John begins his story with Jesus' baptism, but he has a longer introduction which explains in poetic language the relationship between Jesus and God:

In the beginning the Word already existed; the Word was with God, and the Word was God. From the very beginning the Word was with God. Through him God made all things; not one thing in all creation was made without him. The Word was the source of life, and this life brought light to the people. The light shines in the darkness, and the darkness has never put it out.
John 1:1–5

In the account by John, John the Baptist (not the same John!) did not give any sign of having met Jesus before. John knew he was getting people ready for God's chosen one, but it seemed he had no idea who that person was . . . not until he actually baptized Jesus. Then, according to the Gospel writer, John the Baptist had a vision:

"I saw the Spirit come down like a dove from heaven and stay on him. I still did not know that he was the one, but God, who sent me to baptize with water, had said to me, 'You will see the Spirit come down and stay on a man; he is the one who baptizes with the Holy Spirit.' I have seen it. . . . I tell you that he is the Son of God."
John 1:32–34

John baptized Jesus in the River Jordan.

What happened to John

John's Gospel tells of John the Baptist's reaction when he heard of how Jesus was becoming a popular teacher. John's followers came and told him that Jesus was baptizing people and gaining even more followers than John. John the Baptist said this was how things had to be, for Jesus was more important.

The death of John the Baptist

John continued to speak out fearlessly about right and wrong. He even told the local ruler, Herod Antipas (son of the King Herod who had rebuilt the Temple), that he had done wickedly in marrying the wife of his brother, Philip. For this John was thrown into prison.

John was thrown into prison for criticizing the local king.

Herod's wife, Herodias, schemed to have John killed. At Herod's birthday party, the daughter of Herodias, Salome, performed such an astonishing exotic dance for the king and his guests that he offered her any reward she wanted. Salome went and asked her mother for advice. She told her daughter to ask for John the Baptist's head on a plate. The outspoken prophet was duly executed.

John's death was something Jesus and his followers knew about and mourned. It was also a sharp reminder that speaking out as a prophet was a dangerous thing to do.

The king's wife was the one who most wanted John dead, and she schemed with her beautiful daughter, Salome, to make this happen.

Herod's kingdom

John the Baptist and Jesus were born when the cruel king Herod the Great, the rebuilder of the Temple, ruled the land for the Romans. When he died, his kingdom was divided among his three sons: Philip, Herod Antipas, and Archelaus. Archelaus was such a bad ruler that the emperor soon put his region into the charge of a Roman prefect.

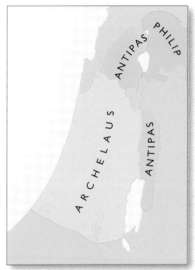

These regions show how Herod's kingdom was divided among his sons.

9 Announcing Jesus: Matthew's Account

Matthew and the Scriptures

In the story of Jesus' birth and throughout his Gospel, Matthew takes every opportunity to show the links between Jesus and the old Scriptures. Through Jesus, Matthew claims, the words of the prophets are being fulfilled.

The star in the east

In modern times, astrologers have tried to work out if there really was a new star in the skies around the time Jesus was born. Various suggestions have been made about planets or comets that may have made a dazzling appearance. Other people are less concerned to find out if there is a scientific background to the story. They are more interested in the way the story shows that Jesus was recognized as a king by people from other lands right from the time he was born.

Matthew, like Mark, announces the start of Jesus' grown-up life with the story of his baptism. However, his Gospel begins with a long list of the ancestors of Jesus all the way back to Abraham, the father of the Jewish nation. The list also names King David and his son King Solomon as ancestors of Jesus, making it clear to his readers that Jesus is of royal descent.

Then he tells of Jesus' birth. A woman named Mary found that she was pregnant. This was something everyone would have been ashamed of, because she was not yet married. Worse, the man she was supposed to marry, Joseph, was not the father. He planned to break off the engagement.

In a dream, an angel told him to go ahead with the wedding. The baby was God's and would save people from their sins.

The baby, Jesus, was born in Bethlehem, the home town of King David. The event was told in the skies, and travelers from lands in the east followed a star in search of a king. They first went to the nearby city of Jerusalem, where Herod the Great was ruling. Herod was furious to hear rumors of a new king. He asked his advisers if there were any clues in the writings of the people as to where the Messiah would be born. They told him, "Bethlehem."

Herod sent the visitors to find the king and told them to report back. They found the baby and gave rich gifts. However, in a dream, an angel warned them to go home without going back to Herod. Joseph was warned to escape with his wife and baby to Egypt.

When Herod found out that the travelers had not returned to tell him exactly which baby was the king they were looking for, he sent his soldiers to Bethlehem

Herod hoped that the travelers from the east would help him hunt down a rival king.

This picture shows Mary, Joseph, and Jesus escaping to Egypt. Together they are sometimes called the Holy Family.

Gifts for a king

Matthew says that the visitors brought gifts of gold, frankincense, and myrrh.

These are costly goods that show the high respect that the travelers had for the one they believed to be a newborn king.

They are often explained as symbolic gifts: gold for a king, frankincense for a priest, and myrrh, a burial spice, for someone whose death was going to be as important as his life.

with orders to kill all the baby boys under the age of two.

A few years later, Joseph heard that Herod had died. He returned to his homeland, but not to Bethlehem. He was afraid of the new ruler, Herod's son Archelaus, so Joseph took his family on to Nazareth in Galilee.

✝ The wise men

The story of the visit of the wise men has captured the imagination of Christians for many centuries, and the splendor of their visit is a popular subject for Christian art. Sometimes they are referred to as the Magi—a word that indicates a link with the guardians of the worship of the Persian god Ahura Mazda. Other legends say that they were kings, perhaps from different parts of the known world. Because there were three gifts, people often refer to three kings. Ancient tradition has even given them names: Balthazar from Africa, Melchior from Media, and Caspar from Persia.

✝ Epiphany

Epiphany is the name of the church festival that celebrates the coming of the wise men. It comes from a Greek word that means "showing," because Jesus was shown to non-Jews and recognized as a king.

Epiphany falls on January 6. On the same date churches of the Orthodox tradition begin to celebrate Christmas Day. In other churches, Epiphany is the last of the special days of the Christmas season.

This fifteenth-century mosaic shows the adoration of the three kings.

10 Announcing Jesus: Luke's Account

Look It Up

A mighty Savior:
Luke 1

Announcing Jesus:
Luke 1

A mighty Savior

When Zechariah was able to speak at last, after his son John was born, he spoke about his own son (page 18) and the one for whom John would prepare the way:

"Let us praise the Lord, the God of Israel!
He has come to the help of his people and has set them free.
He has provided for us a mighty Savior,
a descendant of his servant David.
He promised through his holy prophets long ago
that he would save us from our enemies,
from the power of all those who hate us."

Luke 1:68–71

Luke spends more time than any other Gospel writer on stories about events that happened before the grown-up Jesus was baptized. He begins his book with two birth stories: of John the Baptist and Jesus.

First, Zechariah was told by an angel that he and Elizabeth were to have a baby. The baby would be called John, and he would become a prophet.

While Elizabeth was still pregnant, her cousin Mary received astonishing news from an angel. The angel, Gabriel, said this:

"Don't be afraid, Mary; God has been gracious to you. You will become pregnant and give birth to a son, and you will name him Jesus. He will be great and will be called the Son of the Most High God.
The Lord God will make him a king, as his ancestor David was, and he will be the king of the descendants of Jacob forever; his kingdom will never end!"

Luke 1:30–33

✞ Annunciation

The episode in which the angel Gabriel told Mary that she was to be the mother of God's son is known as the Annunciation. The Annunciation is celebrated in many churches on March 25—nine months before the celebration of Jesus' birth at Christmas.

After the angel came to Mary, she went to see her cousin Elizabeth—an event often called the Visitation.

The Annunciation angel is often shown bearing a lily, a symbol of Mary's purity.

Mary found it hard to believe this: although she was planning to marry a man named Joseph, she was not yet married and knew she could not be pregnant. The angel said that God would make everything come true, and reminded her that her cousin Elizabeth had become pregnant even though everyone thought she was too old to have a child.

Mary went to visit Elizabeth, who at once felt the not-yet-born John leap with joy inside her. Elizabeth declared that this happened because he sensed that Mary's baby was the One promised by God. Then Mary praised God:

Mary and Elizabeth talked about the babies they were expecting.

"My heart praises the Lord;
my soul is glad because of God my Savior,
for he has remembered me, his lowly servant!
From now on all people will call me happy,
because of the great things the Mighty God has done for me.
His name is holy;
from one generation to another
he shows mercy to those who honor him. . . .
He has filled the hungry with good things,
and sent the rich away with empty hands.
He has kept the promise he made to our ancestors,
and has come to the help of his servant Israel.
He has remembered to show mercy to Abraham
and to all his descendants forever!"

Luke 1:46–50, 53–55

✚ Mary of Nazareth

The Gospels do not give very much information about Mary, other than that she was a young girl who was betrothed. This meant that a marriage had been arranged between her family and that of her husband-to-be. It seems she had just reached the age at which the marriage could be completed. In keeping with the customs of the day, she would have been about twelve and her husband-to-be a few years older. She probably lived at home with her parents.

The Gospels say nothing about her parents, but there is an ancient tradition that their names were Joachim and Anne.

✚ Hail, Mary

The first words the angel said to Mary are widely translated as "Hail, Mary." In Latin, this is "Ave, Maria." These words form the opening of a prayer used by many Christians, and particularly those from the Catholic traditions. They say the Hail, Mary when using a string of prayer beads known as a rosary. At the same time, they meditate upon events in Jesus' life.

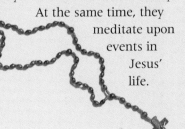

✚ Magnificat

Mary is highly respected by all Christians. The song of praise she sings to God when she is reassured by Elizabeth that her pregnancy is good news is said or sung in many churches. This song is widely known as the *Magnificat,* from the first word of the Latin translation.

11 Luke's Story Continues

Look It Up

Choirs of angels:
Psalms 147–50

Jesus' birth:
Luke 2, also Matthew 1

By the time Elizabeth's son, John, was born, the time for Mary's baby to be born was quite near. Then an announcement from the Roman emperor Caesar Augustus changed everyone's plans. The emperor wanted to conduct a census throughout the empire so he could tax people more effectively. Everyone had to go to their home town to put their names on a register.

Luke says that Mary's husband-to-be, Joseph, was descended from King David, and so his home town was Bethlehem. Mary and Joseph traveled there together. The town was crowded, for many people were having to journey there. The only place Mary and Joseph could find shelter was in a room normally used by animals. There, Mary's baby was born, and she cradled him in a manger. That night, on the hills nearby, shepherds were out watching over their flocks. Suddenly, an angel appeared in a terrifying blaze of light and made a startling announcement:

"Don't be afraid! I am here with good news for you, which will bring great joy to all the people. This very day in David's town your Savior was born—Christ the Lord! And this is what will prove it to you: you will find a baby wrapped in cloths and lying in a manger."

Luke 2:10–12

✚ Choirs of angels

There are several places in the Bible that talk about angels singing praises to God. Some are in the book of Psalms, along with lists of the musical instruments suitable for praising God—trumpets, harps, flutes, drums, and cymbals. As a result, the angels who appear to the shepherds are often depicted in church art singing and playing.

Then a whole crowd of angels appeared, singing:

"Glory to God in the highest heaven, and peace on earth to those with whom he is pleased!"

Luke 2:14

The baby in the manger

Luke's story tells us that Mary wrapped her baby in the traditional way: in swaddling bands. These are strips of cloth that are wound round a baby so as to encase them safely and snugly in a bundle.

The manger may well have been a stone trough—a sturdy little bed that could be made cozy and warm.

When the angels had gone, the shepherds hurried to Bethlehem and found everything just as the angel had said.

✚ Church art and angels

The writings about Jesus make a number of references to angels, but give few clues about what they look like. All that can be said is that people seem to recognize that they are seeing an angel and that the sight is at first terrifying. There is something of heaven about them—the "glory of God." Some angels are described as "dressed in white."

Over the centuries, Christian art has often depicted angels as young and beautiful people with wings and shining haloes, dressed either in white or in rich, jeweled clothing.

A picture of an angel from a medieval Italian church.

✚ Christmas

Jesus' birth is remembered at the festival of Christmas. Many Christians celebrate Christmas on December 25, but those who belong to the Orthodox Church celebrate the festival on January 7.

One popular tradition is to meet for a service as December 24 becomes December 25 and to celebrate Jesus' birth at midnight. There are many other traditions designed to remember the Gospel stories of the birth—the Nativity. There may be Nativity models or crib scenes, Nativity plays, or Nativity pageants.

12   The Boy Jesus Goes to the Temple

Look It Up

Simeon's prophecy:
Luke 1, 2

Jesus in the Temple:
Luke 2

Learning the Law:
Deuteronomy 6

Simeon's prophecy

The Angel Gabriel told Mary she must call her baby "Jesus," and the naming ceremony took place a week after he was born. Later, Mary and Joseph took their infant son to the Temple to dedicate him to God, as the Law required. While they were there, an old man named Simeon asked to hold the child. "Now I am ready to die in peace," he said. "I have seen the one who will bring God's salvation to the people."

After this event, Luke says that Mary and Joseph went back to Nazareth.

✝ Nunc dimittis

Simeon's declaration that he is now ready to die in peace begins in Latin with the words *Nunc dimittis*. His words are often said or sung in churches at evening services and at funerals.

Luke's Gospel is the only one that says anything about Jesus growing up.

Every year, Luke tells us, Jesus' parents traveled to Jerusalem to celebrate the Passover festival at the Temple. When Jesus was twelve, he was allowed to go with them, traveling, as usual, with a party of family and friends.

Once the festival was over, the group set off to return home. Mary and Joseph were confident that Jesus was enjoying himself with friends of his own, and they walked a whole day before they began wondering exactly where he was. They began asking around the group, but no one had seen Jesus.

Frantic with worry, Mary and Joseph hurried back to Jerusalem. They hunted high and low for him. On the third day, they found him in the Temple, sitting with the Jewish teachers. He was listening to what they had to say about their faith and asking questions. Everything Jesus said was wise and showed great understanding.

Mary and Joseph came looking for Jesus.

The teachers of the Law and the priests liked to meet in the Temple courtyard to discuss God's laws. They were surprised at Jesus' understanding.

Mary rushed to scold Jesus for leaving them and making them worry so much. Jesus was surprised. "Why did you have to look for me?" he asked. "Didn't you know that I had to be in my Father's house?" Then he returned home and was an obedient son as before.

Jesus would probably have learned to write words from the Law on wax tablets similar to this.

Learning the Law

In the time of Jesus, boys would have learned the Law at the synagogue school. The Hebrew writing on the wax tablet above is a famous quote from the Jewish Scriptures called the Shema, from the Hebrew word with which it begins:

Hear, O Israel,
the Lord is our God,
the Lord alone.

Here is a clearer version of the schoolboy handwriting used:

Hebrew letters are written from right to left. Children learned to write by hanging them from a line—the opposite of writing them on top of a line as happens with English.

13 Jesus' New Beginning

Look It Up

Jesus' temptation:
Matthew 4, also Mark 1, Luke 4

The hidden years

Apart from Luke's story of the boy Jesus in the Temple, the Gospels say very little about Jesus' early years. It seems there was nothing special to talk about. The townspeople of Nazareth did not think of Jesus as unusual in any way. They knew that he was Mary's son, although there were hints that her husband, Joseph the carpenter, was not his real father.

Nazareth is a very ordinary town to this day. In the time of Jesus, no one thought of Nazareth as the place from which a great leader might come.

Like all boys, Jesus would have been raised to learn his father's trade—as a carpenter and builder. When he was about thirty, he made a dramatic change. According to Matthew, Mark, and Luke, after he was baptized by John, he went off by himself to a lonely place in the wilderness.

The kind of tools used by carpenters in Jesus' day were surprisingly similar to handtools used to this day: items such as saws, chisels, and planes.

As a carpenter and builder in a small town, Jesus would probably have helped construct houses and make farm implements. In this picture a carpenter is using a bow drill to make holes in which to insert the metal teeth for a sledge. The toothed sledge shown against the wall was something used for threshing.

Then the Spirit led Jesus into the desert to be tempted by the Devil. After spending forty days and nights without food, Jesus was hungry. Then the Devil came to him and said, "If you are God's Son, order these stones to turn into bread."

But Jesus answered, "The Scripture says, 'Human beings cannot live on bread alone, but need every word that God speaks.'"

Then the Devil took Jesus to Jerusalem, the Holy City, set him on the highest point of the Temple, and said to him, "If you are God's Son, throw yourself down, for the Scripture says,

'God will give orders to his angels about you;

they will hold you up with their hands,

so that not even your feet will be hurt on the stones.'"

Jesus answered, "But the Scripture also says, 'Do not put the Lord your God to the test.'"

Then the Devil took Jesus to a very high mountain and showed him all the kingdoms of the world in all their greatness. "All this I will give you," the Devil said, "if you kneel down and worship me."

Then Jesus answered, "Go away, Satan! The Scripture says, 'Worship the Lord your God and serve only him!'"

Then the Devil left Jesus; and the angels came and helped him.

Matthew 4:1–11

Jesus thought hard about the choices open to him. He clearly believed he had power that he could use. He could use his power to provide food—putting his own comfort first. He could be a spectacular wonder worker; he could be a great ruler. Jesus knew that his calling was different. He knew the Scriptures well, and he knew what they were saying to him.

In the wilderness

The wilderness where Jesus went was a parched and barren place. Bandits and rebels hid among the caves. Wild animals lurked in the shadows, including snakes, jackals, wolves, and even bears and lions.

✝ Lent

Christians remember the forty days Jesus spent alone in the wilderness in the weeks before Easter. The period is known as Lent. It is traditionally a time of fasting, though this usually means going without rich foods rather than all foods! It is also a period when Christians try to spend extra time praying and reading the Bible.

A bowl of ashes and sackcloth bookmarks are part of Lenten traditions.

A bowl of ashes is part of some traditional church ceremonies for the beginning of Lent, "Ash Wednesday." The person leading the service dips their thumb into the ash and makes the sign of the cross on the forehead of each of the worshipers.

It recalls two things: the ancient Jewish tradition of wearing sackcloth and covering one's head in ashes as a sign of repentance; and the cross of Jesus, which reminds Christians of God's forgiveness.

14 Jesus' New Message

Look It Up

The rejected prophet:
Luke 4, Matthew 13, also Mark 6

The Jesus prayer:
Luke 18

Indoors and outdoors

Jesus is often portrayed preaching to crowds out of doors, often by the shore of Lake Galilee or on the hills around. Indeed, one very famous set of his teachings is known as the Sermon on the Mount. However, the Gospels also say that he preached in the synagogues, where it was quite usual to invite a visiting religious teacher to speak. Other times, people invited him into their homes and he preached to the crowds that gathered—both invited guests and others.

This hillside overlooking Galilee is believed to be one of the places where Jesus preached.

According to Luke, Jesus began preaching in his local synagogue, in Nazareth. It was quite usual that, as one of the local community, he should be asked to read from the Scriptures. He was handed the book of the prophet Isaiah and read this passage:

"The Spirit of the Lord is upon me,
because he has chosen me to bring good news to the poor.
He has sent me to proclaim liberty to the captives
and recovery of sight to the blind,
to set free the oppressed and announce that the time
has come when the Lord will save his people."
Luke 4:18–19

As he sat down, Jesus said that the prophecy had just come true. His listeners were angry: they could not believe the young man they thought they knew so well could be a prophet. Angrily, they threw him out.

The rejected prophet

Mark and Matthew also tell the story of Jesus being thrown out of Nazareth, but the story comes later on in their account. The people of Nazareth make this complaint:

"Where did he get such wisdom?" they asked. "And what about his miracles? Isn't he the carpenter's son? Isn't Mary his mother, and aren't James, Joseph, Simon, and Judas his brothers? Aren't all his sisters living here? Where did he get all this?" And so they rejected him.

Jesus said to them, "A prophet is respected everywhere except in his hometown and by his own family."

Matthew 13:54–57

These ruins of a synagogue at Capernaum stand on the foundations of an earlier building—perhaps the synagogue that Jesus knew.

✝ Sin

Mark announced Jesus' message clearly and simply: "The right time has come and the kingdom of God is near! Turn away from your sins and believe the Good News!"

The word *sin* is used today to mean a range of things. When Jesus talks about sin, it simply means falling short of God's standards of love, justice, and peace.

Through the centuries, there has been a Christian tradition of confessing one's sins to God and asking for God's forgiveness. The most frequently used prayer of confession is sometimes known as the Jesus prayer:

God have mercy on me, a sinner.

These are the words said by someone in one of Jesus' parables—which you can read on page 63.

✝ Liberation

The words Jesus read from Isaiah say that his message of good news includes bringing liberty and justice. In the twentieth century, some Christians began focusing on what became known as "Liberation theology." This movement is concerned with the sins—or wrongdoing—that an individual might commit. It is also passionate about bringing changes to society that enable everyone to live freely and have fair opportunities.

These Filipino Christians believe it is right to use guerilla tactics to win justice for the very poor.

15 In Capernaum

These remains of a house from around the time of Jesus have been unearthed in Capernaum. They are known as the house of St. Peter. Sadly, there is no real evidence that it definitely belonged to Peter.

A healing in Capernaum

One day, when Jesus first went to stay with his friend Simon, Simon's mother-in-law was sick with a fever. Jesus went to her bedside. By a miracle he made her well, and she was able to take care of her guest.

By that evening, the news had spread. Crowds gathered, bringing sick people with them, and Jesus healed them all.

After Jesus was rejected at Nazareth, he went a few miles away to the lakeside fishing town called Capernaum. He was welcomed into the home of a young fisherman, Simon.

He began to get noticed because he could heal people of all kinds of illnesses with just a touch. Crowds soon gathered as he traveled to nearby places, preaching in the synagogues.

Jesus also began to gather a group of followers—disciples.

As Jesus walked along the shore of Lake Galilee, he saw two fishermen, Simon and his brother Andrew, catching fish with a net. Jesus said to them, "Come with me, and I will teach you to catch people." At once they left their nets and went with him.

He went a little farther on and saw two other brothers, James and John, the sons of Zebedee. They were in their boat getting their nets ready. As soon as Jesus saw them, he called them; they left their father Zebedee in the boat with the hired men and went with Jesus.

Mark 1:16–20

John's story of the fishermen

John tells the story of Jesus calling the fishermen in a different way from Mark. In his Gospel, John the Baptist sees Jesus and tells two of his own disciples that Jesus is God's chosen one. They follow Jesus and spend an afternoon listening to him. One of them is Andrew, and he then goes to fetch his brother Simon, telling him that he has found the Christ, the Messiah. When Jesus sees Simon, he gives him a nickname—Peter, the word meaning "rock." Soon after, Jesus calls Philip, who clearly believes that Jesus is sent by God. Philip in turn calls Nathanael to join them.

Some of Jesus' closest friends were fishermen. The work was hard, but it made a decent living. They took a great risk in giving up their jobs to follow Jesus.

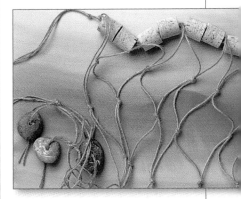

This reconstruction of a fishing net from the time of Jesus shows a row of floats along the top edge and a row of weights along the bottom edge. These would have helped the net to hang vertically in the water between two fishing boats, rather like a submerged fence. As the boats moved it through the water, fish would have been caught in it.

16 Followers and Disciples

Look It Up

The tax collector:
Mark 2, also Matthew 9, Luke 5

Following Jesus:
Luke 8, 9, 12, 14, also Matthew 8, 10

The twelve disciples:
Luke 6, also Matthew 10, Mark 3

As close as family:
Mark 3, also Matthew 12, Luke 8

The tax collector

One day, Jesus was preaching to a crowd, when he saw a tax collector named Levi. He called Levi to follow him, and at once the man left his desk in the marketplace. Tradition says that this Levi is the same person as the Gospel writer, Matthew.

Jesus seemed pleased to welcome people to be his followers, whatever their background. The Pharisees taught that it was wrong to associate with certain kinds of people, such as tax collectors and outcasts, and they criticized Jesus for doing so.

These silver coins show the Roman emperors Tiberius and Augustus. People had to pay taxes to the Roman rulers and tax collectors were hated for collaborating with the Romans.

When people heard Jesus' parable about the person who wanted to build a tower, they may well have thought of something like this. These watchtowers were built in the corner of vineyards. As the grapes ripened, workers would keep watch day and night to make sure no one came to steal the crop.

Jesus' first disciples were four fishermen: Peter and Andrew, James and John. However, Jesus soon invited other people to follow him, while many others came of their own accord.

After a while, Jesus chose twelve disciples to be his closest helpers and companions. He spent a night in prayer before choosing them.

However, there were many other followers of Jesus. Luke refers to a number of women. A woman named Mary Magdalene (because she came from Magdala) was grateful to Jesus because he had cured her of some illness, described as "seven demons." Joanna was the wife of a government official, and she, along with someone called Susanna and many others gave their own money to help support Jesus and his disciples.

The cost of following Jesus

Jesus gave stern warnings to some of his would-be followers that it was going to be a big commitment. He told this parable:

"If one of you is planning to build a tower, you sit down first and work out what it will cost, to see if you have enough money to finish the job. If you don't, you will not be able to finish the tower after laying the foundation; and all who see what happened will make fun of you. 'You began to build but can't finish the job!' they will say."

Luke 14:28–30

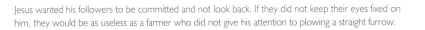

Jesus wanted his followers to be committed and not look back. If they did not keep their eyes fixed on him, they would be as useless as a farmer who did not give his attention to plowing a straight furrow.

Jesus warned that his followers would have to be ready to face criticism and even punishment for spreading his message, and that God would help them:

"When they bring you to be tried in the synagogues or before governors or rulers, do not be worried about how you will defend yourself or what you will say. For the Holy Spirit will teach you at that time what you should say."

Luke 12:11–12

They would have to be prepared to give up their possessions and let their family take second place.

As they went on their way, a man said to Jesus, "I will follow you wherever you go."

Jesus said to him, "Foxes have holes, and birds have nests, but the Son of Man has nowhere to lie down and rest."

He said to another man, "Follow me."

But that man said, "Sir, first let me go back and bury my father."

Jesus answered, "Let the dead bury their own dead. You go and proclaim the Kingdom of God."

Someone else said, "I will follow you, sir; but first let me go and say goodbye to my family."

Jesus said to him, "Anyone who starts to plough and then keeps looking back is of no use to the kingdom of God."

Luke 9:57–62

The twelve disciples

Jesus' close followers are called disciples, from a word meaning "pupil." The names of the twelve are as follows:

Simon Peter and his brother Andrew
James and his brother John
Philip and Bartholomew
Matthew and Thomas
James
Simon the Patriot
Judas (but Matthew and Mark have Thaddeus)
Judas Iscariot

As close as family

On one occasion, Jesus' family came to see him when he was busy teaching. They were afraid he had gone mad and wanted to take him home. When Jesus heard that they had come to see him he said this:

"Who is my mother? Who are my brothers?" He looked at the people sitting round him and said, "Look! Here are my mother and my brothers! Whoever does what God wants him to do is my brother, my sister, my mother."

Mark 3:33–35

Son of Man

Jesus often referred to himself as the Son of Man. Christians have many ideas about what this means, but one simple meaning is "an ordinary man."

17  Miracles

According to Matthew, Mark, and Luke, Jesus began working miracles of healing as soon as he became a preacher. John tells a different story of his first miracle. He says it helped the disciples to believe in Jesus.

The wedding at Cana

There was a wedding in the town of Cana in Galilee. Jesus' mother was there, and Jesus and his disciples had also been invited.

At a Jewish wedding the bride and groom sit under a special canopy while merrymaking goes on all around.

Look It Up

The wedding at Cana:
John 2

Water jars

The kind of jars mentioned in the story of the water into wine were huge—big enough to hold 100 liters of water. Servants would probably have had to make several journeys from the well with smaller pitchers of water in order to fill them.

Large stone jars of this kind were found among the ruins of a first-century house in Jerusalem. Standing up to 80 cm tall, they were cut from a huge block of stone and turned on a lathe to give them a pedestal foot and simple line decorations. They may well have had flat lids to keep dust and insects out.

Making wine

In the time of Jesus, the wine-making process was shared by the community. Few farmers could have afforded a wine press of their own. Instead, everyone shared the same one, and pressing the grapes was a time for feasting and fun.

This wine press works by stacking baskets of grapes to squeeze the juice out. Other wine presses consisted of a pit where workers trod the grapes.

Then the host ran out of wine. What an embarrassment! Jesus' mother came and told him the problem.

"You must not tell me what to do," replied Jesus. "My time has not yet come."

Mary was sure that Jesus would do something, and she told the servants to do whatever he asked.

There were six huge stone jars in the house—tubs for holding bathing water, about 100 liters each. "Fill them with water," Jesus told the servants. So they did.

"Now take some of the water and give it to the man in charge of the feast." They did so. The man tasted it, and at once called the bridegroom over. "Wonderful," he said to him. "Everyone else serves the best wine first, and after the guests have had plenty to drink, makes do with ordinary wine. But you have kept the best wine until now."

✛ The right use of wine

Wine was an everyday drink in the time of Jesus. However, the Bible criticizes drunkenness. As a result, some groups of Christians refuse to drink alcohol while others even include it in their communion services.

18  Miracles of Healing

Look It Up

God's power over evil:
Luke 9, also Matthew 17, Mark 9

Outcasts and outsiders:
Luke 17

Evil spirits

Jesus lived in a time when evil spirits were thought to be the reason for all kinds of disorders. Today, doctors might describe some of those disorders in a different way. However, everyone would agree that something bad was getting in the way of the person living a full and happy life. Jesus got rid of that badness.

Leprosy

Some translations of the Gospels use the word *leprosy* for the skin disease that made people outcasts. Many people now think that this was not the same disease as the one that is today known as leprosy. Even so, the link between Jesus and leprosy has inspired many Christians over the centuries to use medical skills to help cure the disease.

Many of Jesus' miracles are miracles of healing. However, the stories are often about something more than the body being made healthy again.

God's power over evil

The Gospels often talk about Jesus telling evil spirits to leave people alone. Here is one:

A man shouted from the crowd, "Teacher, I beg you, look at my son—my only son! A spirit attacks him with a sudden shout and throws him into a fit, so that he foams at the mouth; it keeps on hurting him and will hardly let him go! I begged your disciples to drive it out, but they couldn't."

Jesus answered, "How unbelieving and wrong you people are! How long must I stay with you? How long do I have to put up with you?" Then he said to the man, "Bring your son here."

As the boy was coming, the demon knocked him to the ground and threw him into a fit. Jesus gave a command to the evil spirit, healed the boy, and gave him back to his father. All the people were amazed at the mighty power of God.

Luke 9:38–43

A father begged Jesus to heal his son.

Outcasts and outsiders

In the time of Jesus, people who suffered from some diseases were treated as outcasts. Jesus healed many such people, showing that he wanted them to be brought back into the community.

In one story, the outcast who was healed was also an outsider. In this case, it was a Samaritan. Samaritans were people who lived in a neighboring region. Most Jews despised them because they thought they had wrong beliefs about how to worship God.

As Jesus made his way to Jerusalem, he went along the border between Samaria and Galilee. He was going into a village when he was met by ten men suffering from a dreaded skin disease. They stood at a distance and shouted, "Jesus! Master! Take pity on us!"

Jesus saw them and said to them, "Go and let the priests examine you."

On the way they were made clean.

When one of them saw that he was healed, he came back, praising God in a loud voice. He threw himself to the ground at Jesus' feet and thanked him. The man was a Samaritan. Jesus said, "There were ten men who were healed; where are the other nine? Why is this foreigner the only one who came back to give thanks to God?" And Jesus said to him, "Get up and go; your faith has made you well."

Luke 17:11–19

Only one of the ten men who were healed returned to thank Jesus.

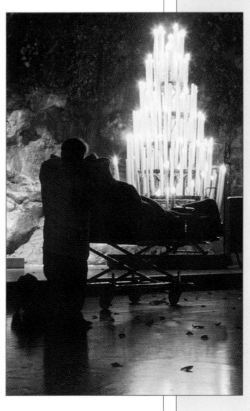

A person who cannot walk is wheeled into the grotto at Lourdes.

Through the centuries, many Christians have been committed to continuing Jesus' work of healing the sick. They have often been involved in setting up hospitals and working in medical professions. To this day, Christians are often found among those who bring medical aid to places ravaged by war, famine, and disaster.

Many Christians also believe in God's power to heal illness by a miracle. Some make a special pilgrimage to places known for miraculous healings, and sometimes actual healing does take place. The most famous place of pilgrimage is Lourdes, in France. Even those who are not healed physically often say they are comforted by their experiences of God's love during the pilgrimage.

19 Miracles and the Law

The kind of house where a crowd could gather was probably a cluster of buildings around a courtyard. Steps led up to a flat roof made from rafters criss-crossed with branches and packed with mud plaster. It would have needed constant repairs.

The flat roof was a useful part of the house—a place to store things and a place to sit and relax. There was a law that it must have a low wall or parapet so people didn't fall off.

Jesus' power to work miracles soon brought him into serious disagreement with the religious leaders.

Jesus went back to Capernaum, and the news spread that he was at home. So many people came together that there was no room left, not even out in front of the door. Jesus was preaching the message to them when four men arrived, carrying a paralyzed man to Jesus. Because of the crowd, however, they could not get the man to him. So they made a hole in the roof right above the place where Jesus was. When they had made an opening, they let the man down, lying on his mat. Seeing how much faith they had, Jesus said to the paralyzed man, "My son, your sins are forgiven."

Some teachers of the Law who were sitting there thought to themselves, "How does he dare to talk like this? This is blasphemy! God is the only one who can forgive sins!"

At once Jesus knew what they were thinking, so he said to them, "Why do you think such things? Is it easier to say to this paralyzed man, 'Your sins are forgiven,' or to say, 'Get up, pick up your mat, and walk'? I will prove to you, then, that the Son of Man has authority on earth to forgive sins." So he said to the paralyzed man, "I tell you, get up, pick up your mat, and go home!"

While they all watched, the man got up, picked up his mat, and hurried away.

Mark 2:1–12

Keeping the Sabbath

Religious Jews were very careful to follow their laws. One of the ten commandments said that no one was to work on the weekly day of rest, the Sabbath. Teachers of the Law—many of whom were Pharisees—had tried to describe what this meant down to the last detail. Jesus did something different:

Then Jesus went back to the synagogue, where there was a man who had a paralyzed hand. Some people were there who wanted to accuse Jesus of doing wrong; so they watched him closely to see whether he would heal the man on the Sabbath. Jesus said to the man, "Come up here to the front." Then he asked the people, "What does our Law allow us to do on the Sabbath? To help or to harm? To save someone's life or to destroy it?"

But they did not say a thing. Jesus was angry as he looked around at them, but at the same time he felt sorry for them, because they were so stubborn and wrong. Then he said to the man, "Stretch out your hand." He stretched it out, and it became well again. So the Pharisees left the synagogue and met at once with some members of Herod's party, and they made plans to kill Jesus.

Mark 3:1–6

Power from God

John's Gospel tells of an important miracle after which Jesus fell out with the Pharisees.

There was a man who had been born blind. Jesus put some mud on his eyes, and when the man washed it away, he could see—for the first time ever.

Neighbors took the man to the Pharisees to explain what had happened, but they became very angry. They argued that Jesus could not have cured him because he was a sinner who did not keep the law about the Sabbath. The man clung to his story that Jesus had cured him and said this:

"We know that God does not listen to sinners; he does listen to people who respect him and do what he wants them to do. . . . Unless this man came from God, he would not be able to do a thing."

John 9:31–33

The Pharisees were so angry at this that they threw the man out the synagogue.

Nicodemus

Not all the religious leaders hated Jesus. One, named Nicodemus, went to see Jesus by night. Jesus explained that his message was of God's forgiveness. Some people were so focused on the Law that they too readily condemned those who failed to obey it. Jesus said:

"For God loved the world so much that he gave his only Son, so that everyone who believes in him may not die but have eternal life. For God did not send his Son into the world to be its judge, but to be its savior."

John 3:16–17

For many Christians, the sign of being "born again" is being baptized.

✠ Born again

Jesus also told Nicodemus that if he wanted to be part of God's kingdom he needed to be "born again"— given a new birth by water and God's spirit. Nicodemus himself was puzzled, but since then many Christians use the term as a way of talking about their experience of God's spirit changing their lives.

20 Miraculous Food

Look It Up

Feeding the five thousand:
John 6, also Matthew 14, Mark 6, Luke 9

Feeding the four thousand:
Matthew 15, Mark 8

The Gospel stories say that on more than one occasion, Jesus provided food for great crowds of people by a miracle.

Feeding the five thousand

The Gospel of John tells of a time when a crowd of about five thousand people gathered around Jesus because they had seen his miracles of healing those who were ill. Jesus did not want them to go away hungry, so he asked his disciples where they could get food. The disciples said there was nowhere they could go to buy enough for the crowd, and that they didn't have any money.

A boy offered his packed meal of loaves and fishes to Jesus. People who were out all day often carried their food tied up in a cloth.

Making bread

In the time of Jesus, bread was cooked as flat, round cakes, rather like modern-day pita bread.

The flour was mixed into a dough with salt, oil, yeast, and water and left to rise. Then the dough was punched down and shaped into flat cakes.

This woman is baking bread on the hot wall of a beehive-shaped oven, much as people did in the time of Jesus.

Andrew, who was Simon Peter's brother, said, "There is a boy here who has five loaves of barley bread and two fish. But they will certainly not be enough for all these people."

"Make the people sit down," Jesus told them. (There was a lot of grass there.) So all the people sat down; there were about five thousand men. Jesus took the bread, gave thanks to God, and distributed it to the people who were sitting there. He did the same with the fish, and they all had as much as they wanted.

John 6:8–11

At the end of the meal, the disciples collected twelve baskets of leftovers. Everyone was amazed and wanted Jesus to go on and do more spectacular things and make himself the leader of his people. Jesus refused. He was disappointed that people did not understand his miracles and said:

"Do not work for food that spoils; instead, work for the food that lasts for eternal life."

John 6:27

He explained that he himself was the bread of life. Those who wanted to please God and find eternal life must believe in him. His miracle was not about free food. It was to point to something altogether more important.

Feeding the four thousand

There are separate stories in the Gospels of Matthew and Mark of Jesus feeding four thousand people. These are very similar to the stories of feeding the five thousand. In the miracle of feeding the four thousand, the disciples have seven loaves and a few small fish. At the end, the disciples gather seven baskets of leftovers.

This ancient mosaic of loaves and fishes is found in a church in Galilee.

21 🌴 Bringing Calm

Some of Jesus' miracles show his power over natural forces.

Look It Up

The storm on the lake:
Matthew 8, Mark 4, Luke 8

Walking on water:
Matthew 14, Mark 6, John 6

The power of faith:
Luke 17, also Matthew 17

Dark forces:
Psalms 46

Here is a mosaic from the pavement of the town of Magdala in Galilee, showing a fishing boat. It dates from around the time of Jesus.

The storm on the lake

One evening, Jesus asked his disciples to take them all in a boat to the other side of the lake. Evening was fading into night.

Suddenly a strong wind blew up, and the waves began to spill over into the boat, so that it was about to fill with water. Jesus was in the back of the boat, sleeping with his head on a pillow. The disciples woke him up and said, "Teacher, don't you care that we are about to die?"

Jesus stood up and commanded the wind, "Be quiet!" and he said to the waves, "Be still!" The wind died down, and there was a great calm. Then Jesus said to his disciples, "Why are you so frightened? Have you still no faith?"

The disciples were even more afraid. Who was Jesus if he could make the dark power of the wind and waves obey him?

Walking on water

On another occasion, Jesus' disciples went out in a boat, and Jesus stayed on the shore. Later, it grew stormy, and in the middle of it all, Jesus walked out to rejoin his friends. They saw him walking on the

The picture above is an attempt to show what the Jesus boat would have looked like. The actual hull (seen on the right) has been damaged by time.

The Jesus boat

In 1985, the remains of a boat were found in Lake Galilee. Tests show that it was almost certainly made in the time of Jesus. It may have been sunk during one of the frequent storms on the lake, or it may have been deliberately destroyed a few years after the time of Jesus when Roman soldiers quashed a Jewish rebellion. Whatever the case, it is likely that the boat Jesus sailed in was similar. The boat that has been found was about eight meters long and a little over two meters wide, and made of planks of cedar and oak.

The power of faith

In the story of the storm and the story of walking on water, Jesus seemed surprised that his disciples had no faith. On one occasion, they asked him to make their faith greater and Jesus said this:

"If you had faith as big as a mustard seed, you could say to this mulberry tree, 'Pull yourself up by the roots and plant yourself in the sea!' and it would obey you."

Luke 17:6

It was a way of saying that those who truly trust in God will be able to do amazing things.

Dark forces

The Jewish people were not a seagoing people. Rather, in their storytelling traditions, stormy waters stood for the dark forces of chaos and evil. The story of Jesus calming the storm on the lake would have made listeners think of Jesus as someone who could calm all the wild and terrifying forces in the world.

This psalm from the Hebrew Bible shows a deep-seated belief that God protects people from wild forces:

God is our shelter and strength, always ready to help in times of trouble. So we will not be afraid, even if the earth is shaken and mountains fall into the ocean depths; even if the seas roar and rage, and the hills are shaken by the violence.

Psalms 46:1–3

water and were terrified. Peter asked Jesus to let him walk toward him. For a few steps, Peter also walked on the water. Then he panicked and started to sink. "Save me, Lord!" he cried.

At once Jesus reached out and grabbed hold of him and said, "How little faith you have! Why did you doubt?"

Then they both got into the boat, and the wind died down.

The disciples were amazed. They were convinced that Jesus was the Son of God.

22 Bringing the Dead to Life

Look It Up

Jairus's daughter:
Mark 5, also Matthew 9, Luke 8

Jesus' language:
Mark 5, 7, 15, also Matthew 27

✛ Holy objects

The story on this page tells of a woman who was cured after touching Jesus' cloak. In the Middle Ages, objects that were believed to have been touched by Jesus and by other holy people were thought to have the power to cure anyone who touched them.

Beating death is one thing that humans cannot do. The stories of Jesus raising the dead to life are surely the most astonishing.

Jairus's daughter

There was a man named Jairus, who was an official at his local synagogue. His daughter was seriously ill, and when he heard that Jesus had come to the town he hurried to find him.

Jesus agreed to come and help, but he could not get there quickly because of the crowds. More than that, in the midst of all the pushing and shoving, a woman touched Jesus' cloak, hoping for a cure. Jesus noticed that power had gone out of him and stopped to talk to the woman, healing her of an ailment that had troubled her for many years.

Jairus was beside himself with worry. Why would Jesus not hurry? Then a servant came with the worst possible news: his daughter had died.

"Don't be afraid," said Jesus. "Only believe."

Growing up in the time of Jesus

The gospel account of the raising of Jairus' daughter says that the girl was about twelve. At that age she would hardly have been thought of as a child any more: it was the age at which many girls would have married.

Although boys usually went to school to learn Hebrew and how to read and write, most girls stayed at home and learned the domestic skills they needed. These included such things as preparing meals—grinding corn into flour and growing their own vegetables; fetching water from the well; spinning wool, weaving cloth, and making clothes; taking produce to market and in this way earning more money for the household; and looking after babies and children.

It was traditional in Jesus' day for professional mourners to come and wail at the house where someone had died.

When they reached the house, mourners had already come to sing their wailing songs of grief. Jesus sent them away. He went into the house with Jairus and the girl's mother, and Peter, James, and John.

He went into the room where the child was lying. He took her by the hand and said to her, "Talitha, koum," which means, "Little girl, I tell you to get up."

She got up at once.

Jesus' language

In the story of Jesus' raising Jairus' daughter, the Gospel writer quotes Jesus as saying, "Talitha, koum." There are just a few other references in this Gospel to the actual words Jesus is claimed to have said in his own language. Here is one of the most famous, which Jesus said when he was crucified:

At three o'clock Jesus cried out with a loud shout, "Eloi, Eloi, lema sabachthani?" which means, "My God, my God, why did you abandon me?"

Mark 15:34

The words are in a language known as Aramaic, which is from the same group of languages as Hebrew. This is one reason why most people believe Jesus' everyday language was Aramaic. It is likely that he could also understand some Latin, as that was the official language of the Roman empire. Government officials would have used Latin. However, the language most commonly spoken all over the empire was Greek, so Jesus could probably speak some Greek also.

23  Lazarus

Among Jesus' friends were a household of two sisters, Mary and Martha, and their brother, Lazarus. They lived in a village called Bethany, near Jerusalem.

When Jesus heard that Lazarus was ill, he wanted to go and help him. However, he did not hurry. Then the news came that Lazarus had died. Jesus said to his disciples:

"Lazarus is dead, but for your sake I am glad that I was not with him, so that you will believe."

John 11:14–15

Mary and Martha were amazed to see Lazarus walking out of his tomb.

The purpose of miracles

The Pharisees once came to Jesus and asked him to perform a miracle, "to show that God approved of him." Jesus refused to do so. Yet, in the story of Lazarus, he seemed to be pleased that the disciples saw something that would help them believe. Jesus seemed to be saying that miracles are there to help those with faith, not as a display or show for those who don't have faith.

Funeral customs

The country where Jesus lived has a warm climate, and it was important to bury a body as soon as possible, before it began to rot. It was wrapped in cloth and carried on a stretcher to a tomb.

The tomb was like a cave, with a ledge inside where bodies could be laid and a stone door to seal the entrance when the body was inside.

After a year or more, when the body had decayed, the bones were collected and put into an ossuary.

This stone ossuary is typical of those used at the time of Jesus. It shows the names of Mary and Joseph, but there is no evidence to link it to Jesus' own family.

This picture shows the entrance to what is known as "Lazarus's tomb" and is visited by many pilgrims today. It is like a cave in the rock, with steps going down to an underground chamber.

As they came near, they heard that Lazarus had been buried for four days. Martha came out to meet Jesus and his friends.

Martha said to Jesus, "If you had been here, Lord, my brother would not have died! But I know that even now God will give you whatever you ask him for."

"Your brother will rise to life," Jesus told her.

"I know," she replied, "that he will rise to life on the last day."

Jesus said to her, "I am the resurrection and the life. Those who believe in me will live, even though they die; and those who live and believe in me will never die. Do you believe this?"

"Yes, Lord!" she answered. "I do believe that you are the Messiah, the Son of God, who was to come into the world."

John 11:21–27

Jesus arrived to find Mary weeping and many people trying to comfort the sisters. When Jesus went with them to the tomb, he himself wept.

The tomb was a cave with a stone rolled in front as a door. To everyone's astonishment, he ordered the stone to be removed. Then he called to Lazarus . . . and he came out, wrapped in grave clothes, with a cloth around his face.

Mary and Martha

Luke tells a story of another time when Jesus came to visit Mary and Martha.

Mary sat down at his feet, eager to listen to Jesus' teaching. Martha was left to do all the chores that needed to be done in order to welcome their guests.

When Martha realized that she had been left to struggle on her own, she was furious. She came and demanded that Jesus tell Mary to come and help. Jesus replied:

"Martha! You are worried and troubled over so many things, but just one is needed. Mary has chosen the right thing, and it will not be taken away from her."

Luke 10:41–42

Puzzling parables

What do Jesus' parables mean? He did not explain. In fact, he said that only those who followed him would be able to understand what the parables really meant . . . and even they were often puzzled!

Jesus said, "Listen, then, if you have ears."

Jesus was not particularly concerned that people notice his miracles. He wanted people to listen to what he had to say. He talked of a new kingdom:

"Turn away from your sins, because the Kingdom of heaven is near!"
Matthew 4:17

Sometimes he put it another way, saying,

"I must preach the Good News about the Kingdom of God . . . because that is what God sent me to do."
Luke 4:43

What is the kingdom of heaven?

The kingdom of heaven, said Jesus, is here and now. The people who belonged to it were "those who do what my Father in heaven wants them to do."

Poor people at the rich man's feast.

Living in obedience to God, warned Jesus, was not easy, and not many people would actually do it.

"Go in through the narrow gate, because the gate to hell is wide and the road that leads to it is easy, and there are many who travel it. But the gate to life is narrow and the way that leads to it is hard, and there are few people who find it."
Matthew 7:13–14

The kingdom of heaven

Jesus used lots of different word pictures to help people understand more about the kingdom of heaven. Here are some examples:

Weeds

Jesus said the kingdom of heaven is like a field where a man sowed good seed. In the night, an enemy came and scattered weed seeds. The good plants and the bad plants grew together. Only at harvest time would the good be gathered safely and the bad thrown away.

Yeast

Jesus said the kingdom of heaven is like this: a woman takes a little yeast and mixes it with a lot of flour to make the whole dough rise.

Mustard seed

Jesus said the kingdom of heaven is like a tiny mustard seed. It grows into a huge plant, and birds come and nest in it.

Treasure

Jesus said the kingdom of heaven is like treasure a man finds buried in a field. As soon as he has found it, he covers it up again, then sells everything he has to buy the field.

Pearl

Jesus said the kingdom of heaven is like this: a man is looking for fine pearls. He finds one that is the best he has ever seen, so he goes and sells all he has in order to buy it.

Net

Jesus said that the kingdom of heaven is like fishing. Fishermen cast their nets and pull in their catch. They keep what is good and throw out what is bad.

Jesus told a story to warn his listeners about not responding to God's invitation:

"There was once a man who was giving a great feast to which he invited many people. When it was time for the feast, he sent his servant to tell his guests, 'Come, everything is ready!' But they all began, one after another, to make excuses. The first one told the servant, 'I have bought a field and must go and look at it; please accept my apologies.' Another one said, 'I have bought five pairs of oxen and am on my way to try them out; please accept my apologies.' Another one said, 'I have just gotten married, and for that reason I cannot come.'

"The servant went back and told all this to his master. The master was furious and said to his servant, 'Hurry out to the streets and alleys of the town, and bring back the poor, the crippled, the blind, and the lame.' Soon the servant said, 'Your order has been carried out, sir, but there is room for more.' So the master said to the servant, 'Go out to the country roads and lanes and make people come in, so that my house will be full. I tell you all that none of those who were invited will taste my dinner!'"

Luke 14:16–24

Being like a child

Jesus said that children were naturally at home in the kingdom. One day, some people brought their children to Jesus and asked for Jesus to bless them. The disciples wanted to send them away, saying that Jesus was too busy. Jesus called the people back. He said:

"Let the children come to me and do not stop them, because the Kingdom of heaven belongs to such as these."

Matthew 19:14

25 Those Who Hear and Those Who Do

Look It Up

The parable of the sower:
Matthew 13, also Mark 4, Luke 8

Farmers' fields on the hills that surround Lake Galilee. The people who heard Jesus' parable of the sower would have lived in this kind of landscape, where tall and prickly weeds grow strongly in the stony soil.

Seed is plowed into the ground after it has been scattered.

Jesus said that people who hear about God's kingdom respond in different ways. This story helps explain what he meant.

The parable of the sower

"Once there was a man who went out to sow grain. As he scattered the seed in the field, some of it fell along the path, and the birds came and ate it up. Some of it fell on rocky ground, where there was little soil. The seeds soon sprouted, because the soil wasn't deep. But when the sun came up, it burned the young plants; and because the roots had not grown deep enough, the plants soon dried up. Some of the seed fell among thorn bushes, which grew up and choked the plants. But some seeds fell in good soil, and the plants bore grain; some had one hundred grains, others sixty, and others thirty."

And Jesus concluded, "Listen, then, if you have ears!"

Matthew 13:3–9

This is one parable that Jesus did explain—not to the crowd, but to his disciples.

The seeds represent people who hear Jesus telling about the kingdom.

Some people are like the seeds on the path: they hear the words but do not understand the meaning. The "Evil One" comes and snatches away any kind of understanding they may have had.

Other people are like the seed on rocky ground. They hear the message and understand it. They even begin to live in a new way. However, when things get tough, they give up.

Yet others are like the seed that fell among the thorns. They believe what they hear, but the worries of everyday life and the love of riches mean they don't do anything that really makes a difference.

"And the seeds sown in the good soil stand for those who hear the message and understand it: they bear fruit, some as much as one hundred, others sixty, and others thirty."

Matthew 13:23

Sowing seed

In Jesus' day, sowing seed was done as described in the parable. Here is a rhyme about the farming year based on one that Jesus might have known:

Two months of olive harvest,
Then two months for sowing grain,
Two months to sow the later seeds
All through the winter rain.

A month to hoe the flax
And leave it drying in the sun.
A month to gather barley
Now the harvest has begun.

A month to gather sheaves of wheat
And feast with joy and mirth.
Two months to tend the grapevines
That give wine to all the earth.

A month to gather summer fruits
That ripen in the heat.
Give thanks to God, who made the earth
That gives us food to eat.

The child's rhyme above is adapted from the writing on this stone. It is known as the Gezer calendar and dates back to the time of King David's son Solomon, hundreds of years before the time of Jesus.

26  A Kingdom of Equals

The old laws

The idea that all people are equal in God's eyes was not new. The Scriptures that Jesus and his listeners would have known frequently reminded the people that their ancestors had been slaves and foreigners long ago in Egypt. As a result, they should not look down on those they thought of as outsiders. Even a king should obey this instruction:

"The king . . . is to have a copy of the book of God's laws and teachings. . . . He is to keep this book near him and read from it all his life, so that he will learn to honor the Lord and to obey faithfully everything that is commanded in it. This will keep him from thinking that he is better than other Israelites and from disobeying the Lord's commands in any way."

Deuteronomy 17:17–20

What Jesus says about the kingdom can sometimes be puzzling. However, Christians believe Jesus is telling good news of a God who is unfailingly generous and who treats all people as of equal value. The people who don't like this are those who think they are better than others!

First and last

Jesus said that the kingdom of heaven is like this:

A rich man owned a vineyard. At harvest time, he went down to the marketplace early in the morning to find people who were looking for casual work. He found some and agreed a wage: a silver coin. At nine o'clock, he realized he needed more workers, so he went and hired some more, promising them a fair wage. He did the same at noon, and at three, and then at five.

At six o'clock, it was time to stop working. The men who had been hired at five were given a silver coin. So were all the others, including those who had been hired at the very start of the day. They began grumbling.

The owner answered one of them, "Listen, I have not cheated you. You agreed to do a day's work for one silver coin. Now take your pay and go home. I want to give this man I hired last as much as I have given you. Don't I have the right to do as I wish with my own money? Are you just jealous because I am generous?"

And Jesus concluded, "Those who are last will be first, and those who are first will be last."

Places at a feast

On one occasion, Jesus noticed how some people who were invited to a feast were choosing the best places for themselves. He warned them that this was foolish: perhaps someone who was more important had been invited. They would be ashamed and embarrassed when they had to give up their place. He gave this advice: "When you are invited, go and sit in the lowest places, so that your host will come to you and say, 'Come on up, my friend, to a better place.' This will bring you honor in the presence of all the other guests. For all who make themselves great will be humbled, and those who humble themselves will be made great."

Sons of thunder

The mother of James and John asked Jesus to make sure that her sons would have a position of power in his kingdom. Jesus said that only God could decide. The other disciples were angry that two of their number wanted to be more important. Jesus warned:

"If one of you wants to be great, he must be the servant of the rest; and if one of you wants to be first, he must be the slave of all. For even the Son of Man did not come to be served; he came to serve and to give his life to redeem many people."

Mark 10:43–45

The greatest in the kingdom

One day, the disciples came to Jesus and asked him, "Who is the greatest in the kingdom of heaven?"

Jesus called a child to come and stand in front of them. He told his disciples they would have to become like children even to enter the kingdom:

"The greatest in the Kingdom of heaven is the one who humbles himself and becomes like this child."

Matthew 18:4

In Bible times, children had to make many of their toys and games with the simplest of materials. This board game scratched into a stone slab was played with pebbles.

✛ Living as equals

Because of Jesus' teaching on equality, some groups of Christians do all they can to avoid making some people seem more important in the church than others. Even the people who have special responsibilities are not given titles that sound as if they are greater. They are more likely to talk of one another simply as brother or sister.

These Amish girls are dressed in nearly identical styles. This dress code reflects a desire to live simply and as equals.

Some groups of Christians also have strict rules about lifestyle in an attempt to live as equally as possible. One example is that of Anabaptist groups in North America—the Mennonites, Amish, and Hutterites. Many of them choose to follow the dress code that was first set out in the sixteenth or seventeenth century, with a very limited range of styles and colors. Over the centuries their firm faith and commitment, often in the face of ridicule, has won them great respect.

27 Rich People and the Kingdom

Can a rich person belong to God's kingdom? Not easily, said Jesus. He gave many warnings to wealthy people that riches could easily make them turn away from things that were of lasting value.

"Do not store up riches for yourselves here on earth, where moths and rust destroy, and robbers break in and steal. Instead, store up riches for yourselves in heaven, where moths and rust cannot destroy, and robbers cannot break in and steal. For your heart will always be where your riches are."
Matthew 6:19–21

Who is happy?

Jesus once said:

"Happy are you poor; the Kingdom of God is yours!

Happy are you who are hungry now; you will be filled!

Happy are you who weep now; you will laugh!

. . . But how terrible for you who are rich now; you have had your easy life!

How terrible for you who are full now; you will go hungry!

How terrible for you who laugh now; you will mourn and weep!"

Luke 6:20–21, 24–25

Jesus' rich friends

Jesus did have rich people among his followers. Luke says that there were a number of wealthy women, including Joanna and Susanna, who used their own money to enable Jesus and his disciples to go about their work of preaching and teaching.

The rich young man

One day, a rich young man came to Jesus and asked what he needed to do to have eternal life. On learning that the young man already knew about keeping all God's commandments and living in the right way, Jesus said there was only one more thing he needed to do: sell all he owned and give the money to the poor, and then come and join Jesus and the other followers.

The young man did not feel able to do that. But even Jesus' disciples were shocked at what he said next:

"How hard it will be for rich people to enter the Kingdom of God! . . . It is much harder for a rich person to enter the Kingdom of God than for a camel to go through the eye of a needle."
Mark 10:23–25

58

A parable about riches

Jesus told this story about the dangers of trusting in money.

There was once a rich man. His land produced good crops. Then one thing began to worry him: he didn't have enough barns to store all of his abundant harvests. What could he do? How could he hang on to his wealth?

Then he had an idea. "I'll tear down my old barns and build bigger ones!" he said. "Then I'll be able to say to myself, you lucky man: you have all the good things you need for many years. Take life easy, eat, drink, and enjoy yourself."

But that night, he died. His wealth was no good to him. He was rich in this world, but not rich in the things that matter to God.

The remains of a rich person's mansion from the time of Jesus have been discovered in Jerusalem. The lavish house had elegant rooms and stylish mosaic floors, and the owners could afford fine tableware and glass. No doubt they could dress expensively—perhaps choosing fashions in the Roman style if they wished.

This beautifully decorated pottery is part of the collection of items found in the mansion in Jerusalem. Jesus warned people of becoming too fond of material possessions.

Don't worry

The real problem with being rich, said Jesus, is that it ties people down to worrying about the material world and the things they need and want instead of worrying about the kinds of things that matter to God.

"Look at the birds," said Jesus. "They don't sow and harvest crops. Yet God provides them with the food they need.

"And look at the flowers," said Jesus. "They don't work to make clothes for themselves. Yet the petals they wear for their short time in bloom are finer than anything that even a king could have.

"Instead, be concerned above everything else with the kingdom of God and with what God requires of you, and God will provide you with all these other things."

It took many hours' work to make even simple linen tunics like these—beginning with harvesting the flax plants—yet God clothed the blue flax flowers and the white field daisies with natural loveliness.

28  All About Prayer

Look It Up

The Lord's Prayer:
Luke 11, Matthew 6

The importance of forgiveness:
Matthew 18

The Lord's Prayer

The prayer Jesus taught is the most widely used in the Christian faith. Called the Our Father or the Lord's Prayer, it is said by Christians throughout the world.

Here is one version used today:

Our Father in heaven,
hallowed be your name,
your kingdom come,
your will be done
on earth as in heaven.
Give us today our daily bread.
Forgive us our sins
as we forgive those who sin
*   against us.*
Lead us not into temptation
but deliver us from evil.

There is a traditional ending to the prayer, which has been used by some Christians for many centuries:

For the kingdom, the power, and
the glory are yours, now and forever.
Amen.

The Gospels say Jesus would often get up early in the morning and go out into the countryside. There he would pray: he would spend time talking with God.

Jesus' disciples noticed what he did. Luke tells his readers that Jesus' disciples asked him to teach them to pray, as John the Baptist had taught his disciples. Jesus gave them this prayer:

"Father: May your holy name be honored;
may your kingdom come.
Give us day by day the food we need.
Forgive us our sins,
for we forgive everyone who does us wrong.
And do not bring us to hard testing."
Luke 11:2–4

Matthew gives the same prayer, with just a few differences. It is a short prayer, Jesus explains, but that is enough.

"Our Father in heaven:
May your holy name be honored;
may your kingdom come;
may your will be done on earth as it is in heaven.
Give us today the food we need.
Forgive us the wrongs we have done,
as we forgive the wrongs that others have done to us.
Do not bring us to hard testing,
but keep us safe from the Evil One."
Matthew 6:9–13

At the heart of the prayer is the idea that this world will be God's world, and that everyone will live according to God's standards of right living combined with readiness to confess and to forgive all wrongdoing.

The servant begged for forgiveness and was forgiven.

The importance of forgiveness

One day, Peter came to Jesus and asked him this question: "If someone keeps doing me wrong, how often must I forgive them? Seven times?"

"No," replied Jesus. "Not seven times, but seventy times seven, because the kingdom of heaven is like this:

"There was once a king who decided to check on how much his servants owed him. He discovered that one man owed him millions of pounds. The king asked to see him, and demanded his money back.

"'But I cannot pay!' he pleaded.

"'Then you will be punished,' declared the king. He ordered the man to be sold as a slave, and his wife and children as well.

"'Please be patient,' begged the man. 'Give me time, and I will pay you everything.'

"His tears made the king feel sorry for him. He forgave him the debt and let him go.

"The man went out and found another servant whom he remembered owed him a few pounds. He grabbed him by the throat. 'Pay back what you owe me, and fast,' he demanded.

"'Please be patient,' begged the man. 'Give me time, and I will pay you everything.'

"But the first man was merciless. He had the poor servant thrown into jail.

"When the king found out what had happened, he was very angry. 'You should have had mercy on the man just as I had mercy on you,' he explained. 'But now I shall have you sent to jail until you pay me everything.'"

Jesus concluded, "That is how my father in heaven will treat every one of you unless you forgive your brother from your heart."

✠ Pater Noster

At the place where, many believe, Jesus taught his disciples the Our Father, the words of the prayer are built into the walls of a church. One version is in Latin, which begins with the famous words, "Pater Noster." The church also includes prayers in many different languages from all around the world . . . and there is still room for more.

A man prays by the Ethiopian version of the "Pater Noster."

The forgiven servant was unwilling to forgive others.

29 More About Prayer

Trust in God's goodness

In the Gospel of Matthew, Jesus shows that God is eager to answer prayers. He asks his listeners if the parents among them would ever give their children bad things: "Would any of you give your son a stone when he asks for bread?"

Of course, parents are far from perfect, but they do try to give their children good things. God is far kinder, says Jesus: a loving Father in heaven.

Jesus said there was a right and a wrong way to pray. He gave many examples of this, and he told this parable—in particular for people who were sure of their own goodness and despised everybody else.

"Once there were two men who went up to the Temple to pray: one was a Pharisee, the other a tax collector.

"The Pharisee stood apart by himself and prayed, 'I thank you, God, that I am not greedy, dishonest, or an adulterer, like everybody else. I thank you that I am not like that tax collector over there. I fast two days a week, and I give you a tenth of all my income.'

These two men are praying in an inner courtyard of the Temple in Jerusalem.

"But the tax collector stood at a distance and would not even raise his face to heaven, but beat on his breast and said, 'God, have pity on me, a sinner!'

"I tell you," said Jesus, "the tax collector, and not the Pharisee, was in the right with God when he went home. For all who make themselves great will be humbled, and all who humble themselves will be made great."

Luke 18:10–14

Do not show off

In Jesus' day, some people liked to be noticed when they were praying. They would stand on street corners, with their hands lifted, so everyone would admire them for being so religious. Jesus said that prayer was a private matter. To pray, a person should go off alone, perhaps into their own room, and close the door.

Jewish men covered their heads with a shawl for prayer. The old laws said that these shawls should have a tassel in each corner. Jesus criticized some people for choosing to wear extra long tassels to show off how religious they were.

Two phylacteries. Jewish men tied copies of the Law to their heads by wearing leather phylacteries, which were rather like purses. Inside were tiny scrolls on which words from the Law had been written in minute handwriting. This was to respect the law that told them to tie the laws to their arms and wear them on their foreheads as a reminder. Jesus criticized people who tried to show off by wearing a phylactery that was larger than it needed to be.

✝ Christian prayer

This mural from a Roman British villa shows a Christian believer at prayer. In the early centuries of the faith, people stood to pray, as the Jews did in the time of Jesus and still do today. The present-day tradition of kneeling observed by many Christians is linked to a line from a letter that is now in the New Testament.

*And so, in honor of the name of Jesus
    all beings in heaven, on earth,
    and in the world below
    will fall on their knees,
and all will openly proclaim
    that Jesus Christ is Lord,
    to the glory of God the Father.*

Philippians 2:10–11

In some churches, worshipers bend the knee, or genuflect, when the name of Jesus is mentioned.

30 Jesus' Teaching About Right Living

Clean hands

Some of the Pharisees and teachers of the Law criticized Jesus' followers for eating a meal without having washed their hands. It was not germs they were worried about—they were offended that the religious ritual was being ignored.

Jesus explained that nothing that goes into a person makes him unclean in God's eyes. He said:

"It is what comes out of you that makes you unclean. For from the inside, from your heart, come the evil ideas which lead you to do immoral things, to rob, kill, commit adultery, be greedy, and do all sorts of evil things; deceit, indecency, jealousy, slander, pride, and folly."

Mark 7:20–22

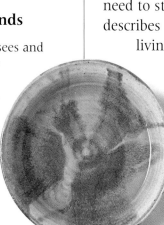

Religious Jews had strict rules about washing—rules which Jesus seemed to take lightly.

At the heart of Jesus' teaching is the good news that God is all-forgiving. However, Jesus also gives very clear teaching about how people should live.

"Do not think that I have come to do away with the Law of Moses and the teachings of the prophets. I have not come to do away with them, but to make their teachings come true."

Matthew 5:17

Love your enemies

The Law, explains Jesus, is rather limited. It tells people about the need to steer clear of wrongdoing, such as murder and adultery; it also describes the fair punishment for those who break those laws. Right living, says Jesus, goes much deeper. Don't just steer clear of killing someone: don't even give way to anger and hatred. Don't just stay away from adultery: make sure that all your relationships are pure. Don't think you're being good if you only demand fair revenge against someone who wrongs you: instead, do good to them.

"You have heard that it was said, 'Love your friends, hate your enemies.' But now I tell you: love your enemies and pray for those who persecute you."

Matthew 5:43–44

Jesus himself showed that he was willing to forgive. Luke's Gospel says that when Jesus hung dying on the cross he prayed for his enemies:

"Forgive them, Father! They don't know what they are doing."

Luke 23:34

Doing good in secret

Right living is not something to show off about, warns Jesus. If you give to the poor, it is right to do so in secret so no one knows. God will notice and God bless the person for their kindness.

Shining goodness

At the same time, true goodness is something that can't be hidden. Righteous people will be like lights in a dark world. Everyone will notice that the people who live as part of God's kingdom make a real difference to the way the world is. As a result, they will praise God.

Words or actions

Not everyone who claims to do good things actually does them, warned Jesus. God will see what a person actually does. He told this story.

The two sons showed their respect for their father by what they actually did.

"Now, what do you think? There was once a man who had two sons. He went to the elder one and said, 'Son, go and work in the vineyard today.' 'I don't want to,' he answered, but later he changed his mind and went. Then the father went to the other son and said the same thing. 'Yes, sir,' he answered, but he did not go. Which one of the two did what his father wanted?"

"The older one," they answered.

So Jesus said to them, "I tell you: the tax collectors and the prostitutes are going into the Kingdom of God ahead of you. For John the Baptist came to you showing you the right path to take, and you would not believe him; but the tax collectors and the prostitutes believed him. Even when you saw this, you did not later change your minds and believe him."

Matthew 21:28–32

✠ **Gifts in secret**

One of the best-loved stories in the Christian tradition is of someone who gave gifts in secret. A bishop in the town of Myra heard of a family of three daughters. They were so poor their father could not afford the marriage dowry they needed. The bishop went to their house in the dark of night and tossed bags of gold inside. Some say he threw the gold in a window; others that he threw it down the chimney where the coins rolled among the shoes and stockings drying by the hearth. The man was Saint Nicholas, who has become famous around the world by a version of his name: Santa Claus. The Christmas tradition of giving secret gifts comes from this legend—and from Jesus' teaching.

Saint Nicholas and the three girls.

31  Who Is My Neighbor?

Look It Up

Love your neighbor:
Luke 10

The great laws:
*Deuteronomy 6, Leviticus 19, Exodus 20,
also Deuteronomy 5*

The story of the Good Samaritan is just a story. Nevertheless, Jesus gives it a real setting between Jerusalem and Jericho. This ancient roadside inn is visited by many pilgrims to remind them of Jesus' story.

The teachers of the Law were intrigued and puzzled by what Jesus said. However, they were suspicious that Jesus was disrespectful of the Law. One day, a teacher of the Law came and tried to trap Jesus by asking him a question that might lure him into saying things that would prove them right.

"Teacher," he asked. "What must I do to receive eternal life?"

Jesus answered him, "What do the Scriptures say? How do you interpret them?"

The man answered, "'Love the Lord your God with all your heart, with all your soul, with all your strength, and with all your mind;' and 'Love your neighbor as you love yourself.'"

"You are right," Jesus replied; "do this and you will live."

But the teacher of the Law wanted to justify himself, so he asked Jesus, "Who is my neighbor?"

The priest and the Levite hurried past the man lying wounded in the road. Jesus' listeners would have understood one reason for their seeming heartlessness: the old laws said that touching a dead body made a person "unclean"—unfit to take part in religious ceremonies until the purification rituals were complete. Jesus' story showed that kindness is more important.

Then Jesus told this parable:

"There was once a man who was going down from Jerusalem to Jericho when robbers attacked him, stripped him, and beat him up, leaving him half dead. It so happened that a priest was going down that road; but when he saw the man, he walked on by on the other side. In the same way a Levite also came there, went over and looked at the man, and then walked on by on the other side. But a Samaritan who was traveling that way came upon the man, and when he saw him, his heart was filled with pity. He went over to him, poured oil and wine on his wounds and bandaged them; then he put the man on his own animal and took him to an inn, where he took care of him. The next day he took out two silver coins and gave them to the innkeeper. 'Take care of him,' he told the innkeeper, 'and when I come back this way, I will pay you whatever else you spend on him.'"

And Jesus concluded, *"In your opinion, which one of these three acted like a neighbor toward the man attacked by the robbers?"*

The teacher of the Law answered, *"The one who was kind to him."*

Jesus replied, *"You go, then, and do the same."*

Luke 10:25–37

The Jewish people believed that Moses had brought the ten commandments from God carved on tablets of stone.

The great laws

The teacher of the Law quoted two Scriptures to answer Jesus:

"Love the Lord your God with all your heart, with all your soul, and with all your strength."

Deuteronomy 6:5

"Love your neighbors as you love yourself."

Leviticus 19:18

These two great laws were a summary of hundreds of other laws. Another famous summary in the Scriptures is the ten commandments, which also contain instructions about loving God and one's neighbor.

• I am the Lord your God. Worship no god but me.
• Do not make images of anything or bow down to idols.
• Do not use my name for evil purposes.
• Keep the Sabbath day holy.
• Respect your father and your mother.
• Do not murder.
• Do not commit adultery.
• Do not steal.
• Do not accuse anyone falsely.
• Do not covet what belongs to someone else.

Samaritans and Jews

Samaritans came from the region known as Samaria. Samaritans had their own religious traditions and did not have the same respect for the Temple in Jerusalem.

For over a century, there had been many bloody skirmishes between Samaritans and Jews.

When Jesus was a boy, there was a serious incident when some Samaritans had scattered bones in the Temple in Jerusalem. This was considered an outrage.

For all these reasons Jews and Samaritans hated each other.

Jesus did not only tell people to show kindness to others. He himself welcomed all kinds of people into his company.

The woman from Samaria

On one occasion, Jesus was traveling through Samaria. In the heat of the day, he sat down to rest by a well in the town of Sychar while his disciples went on to buy food.

A woman came to draw water, and Jesus asked her to give him a drink.

She was shocked: she knew that most Jews would not share the same cups and bowls as Samaritans.

Jesus said to her:

"If only you knew what God gives and who it is that is asking you for a drink, you would ask him, and he would give you life-giving water."
John 4:10

Samaria

Samaria lay between Jesus' home country of Galilee and Judea, where the worship of God was focused on the Temple. Many Jews would take a long detour to avoid traveling through it.

Hills of Samaria.

He stayed to talk with her, even though he knew that she was a woman with a string of broken relationships who was looked down on in her own community.

Jesus also talked about how the great argument between Jews and Samaritans, about where to worship, was no longer important:

"The time is coming and is already here, when by the power of God's Spirit people will worship the Father as he really is, offering him the true worship that he wants."
John 4:23

The woman went to fetch other people from her village, and many came to listen to Jesus and welcomed his message.

The woman with a bad reputation
One day, a Pharisee named Simon invited Jesus to dinner. In a Pharisee's home, every detail of the meal would be done with the utmost care to observe all the laws about food and cleanliness.

In the same town was a woman who had a bad reputation— a prostitute. She heard where Jesus was and went to find him, bringing with her a jar of precious perfume. She was weeping about something, and her tears washed Jesus' feet. Then she poured out the perfume and dried Jesus' feet with her hair.

The Pharisee was appalled. "If this man really were a prophet, he would know who this woman is who is touching him; he would know what kind of sinful life she lives!"

Jesus replied to Simon with a parable. "There were two people who owed money to a moneylender," said Jesus. "One owed him five hundred silver coins, and the other fifty. Neither of them could pay him back, so he canceled the debts of both. Which one, then, will love him more?"

Simon could answer that: the one who had been let off a huge debt would be even more delighted than the one who had been let off a small debt. Jesus explained that the woman's extravagant display of gratitude to Jesus was rather like the delight of someone let off a debt: she knew that she had many sins that needed forgiveness.

Then Jesus told the woman that her sins were forgiven.

Who has never sinned?
John's Gospel includes a story about a time when Jesus was teaching in the Temple in Jerusalem. The teachers of the Law and the Pharisees dragged before him a shamefaced and terrified woman who had been caught committing adultery. They reminded him that according to the Law of Moses the punishment for adultery was being stoned to death. Jesus did not rush to answer.

Then he said:

"Whichever one of you has committed no sin may throw the first stone at her."

One by one, all the accusers went away. Jesus said to the woman:

"Is there no one left to condemn you?"

"No one, sir," she answered.

"Well, then," Jesus said, "I do not condemn you either. Go, but do not sin again."
John 8:1–7, 10–11

Perfume jars from the time of Jesus.

Look It Up

The tax collector:
Luke 19

The centurion:
Matthew 8, also Luke 7

Jericho is built on a natural oasis and is a green, fertile place in otherwise barren country.

Jericho

Jesus' meeting with the tax collector Zacchaeus took place in Jericho. This city—which still exists today—is one of the oldest in the world. It is in a warm and sheltered valley but has springs of fresh water. In the time of Jesus, it was a city where wealthy people from Jerusalem liked to have a second home.

Jesus was a religious teacher, and most religious teachers among the Jews thought that their faith was special to them. Jesus was unusual in the way he dealt with foreigners and even those despised Jewish people who collaborated with the Romans.

The tax collector

On one occasion, as Jesus was making his way to Jerusalem, he passed through the oasis town of Jericho. The chief tax collector there was a man named Zacchaeus. He was very rich, and everyone knew why. He didn't limit himself to collecting taxes for the Romans, with just a little extra to pay his own wages. He cheated people out of far more money than was right.

Zacchaeus wanted to see Jesus, the teacher everyone was talking about. Unfortunately for him, he was very short, and he could not see anything because of the number of people who had gathered to watch. So he ran ahead till he came to a sycamore tree and climbed up.

When Jesus came past, he looked up and called to Zacchaeus. "Come down, Zacchaeus, because I must stay in your house today."

Zacchaeus hurried down, delighted to be so honored. The watching crowd began to grumble. What kind of person was Jesus if he chose to go to the home of someone as despicable as Zacchaeus?

The meeting with Jesus changed the greedy tax collector for ever.

Zacchaeus stood up and said to the Lord, "Listen, sir! I will give half my belongings to the poor, and if I have cheated anyone, I will pay back four times as much."

Jesus said to him, "Salvation has come to this house today. . . . The Son of Man came to seek and to save the lost."

Luke 19:8–10

The centurion

On one occasion, a Roman centurion came to Jesus. His servant was ill, and he wanted Jesus to work a miracle of healing. Jesus was prepared to go to his house, but the soldier said that wasn't necessary: he himself was used to giving orders and knew that what he ordered would always be done. He believed that Jesus could also ask for a miracle and expect it to happen.

Jesus was astonished and delighted that a foreigner had so much faith in God, and the man's servant was healed.

Jesus commented:

"I assure you that many will come from the east and the west and sit down with Abraham, Isaac, and Jacob at the feast in the Kingdom of heaven."

Matthew 8:11

A Roman soldier in chain mail—cooler than plate armor and more suitable for a hot country.

Occupying troops

The occupying troops with their heavy weapons were not popular with the local people. However, some of the soldiers, such as the centurion who came to see Jesus, had respect for the Jewish religion and tried to help the local community.

The fortress of Antonia was the garrison building in Jerusalem— a huge structure rivalling the Temple for grandeur and dominating the dwellings of ordinary people.

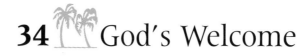

Jesus was happy to talk to anyone—including foreigners and outcasts. The Pharisees and the teachers of the Law did not like this at all. So Jesus told these parables about God's delight when those who were lost are found.

Look It Up

The lost coin:
Luke 15

The loving father and his sons:
Luke 15

The lost sheep:
Luke 15, also Matthew 18

The lost coin

Jesus told a story about a woman who loses a coin in her house. She lights a lamp and sweeps everywhere until she finds it. Then she calls her neighbors around to celebrate with her.

A silver coin called a shekel, from around 30 BCE.

The loving father

There was once a man who had two sons. They worked with him on the family farm. One day, the younger son came to his father with a demand: "I want my share of your property now. I don't want to have to wait till you die."

So the father divided the property, and at once, the younger son sold his share. He took the money and set off for a distant country. There, he enjoyed himself to the full, with every luxury he wanted.

Then famine hit the land. The young man found that his money was quickly gone, and he was left with nothing. In desperation he took a job looking after pigs. He was so hungry, he was even tempted to eat the pigs' food.

From the top of his flat-roofed house, the father in Jesus' story could have seen his son returning from a long way off.

The returning son—referred to as the prodigal son.

The lost sheep

Jesus told this story:

"Suppose a shepherd has a hundred sheep and loses one of them. What does he do? He leaves the other ninety-nine sheep in the pasture and goes looking for the one that got lost until he finds it. When he finds it, he is so happy that he puts it on his shoulders and carries it back home. Then he calls his friends and neighbors together and says to them, 'I am so happy I found my lost sheep. Let's celebrate!'"

Jesus said, "In the same way, there will be more joy in heaven over one sinner who repents than over ninety-nine respectable people who do not need to repent."

At last he came to his senses. "My father's servants live better than this," he said to himself. "I shall go back, admit that I have done wrong and ask to be hired as a servant."

He was still a long way from home when his father saw him; his heart was filled with pity, and he ran to meet his son, threw his arms around him, and kissed him.

"Father," the son said, "I have sinned against God and against you. I am no longer fit to be called your son."

But the father was overjoyed to see his son. "Hurry!" he said to his servants. "Bring him the best clothes and prepare a great feast. For this son of mine was dead, but now he is alive; he was lost, but now he has been found."

The elder brother

Jesus' story says that the elder brother was out working in the fields when his wayward brother returned. As he came wearily home, he was puzzled to hear the sound of music and dancing. When he heard that his father was throwing a party for his brother, he was furious and wouldn't even come into the house. He complained that he had never been treated half as well.

The father tried to calm the brother down, explaining that everything he owned now belonged to him.

One way of understanding the meaning of this episode is that respectable people are often angry when they see the generous way God forgives those who do wrong.

A present-day shepherd takes his flocks to find pastures in the dry and rocky hills of the land where Jesus lived. Those who heard Jesus' parable of the lost sheep would have had this kind of wild country in mind as they imagined a good shepherd searching for his missing animal.

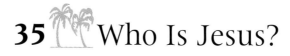

35 Who Is Jesus?

Look It Up

Jesus the Messiah:
Matthew 16, also Mark 8, Luke 9

The transfiguration:
Matthew 17, also Mark 9, Luke 9

Little shrines carved into the rock at Caesarea Philippi.

Caesarea Philippi

Jesus and his disciples were visiting the northern town of Caesarea Philippi when Peter made his declaration that Jesus was the Messiah. In the time of Jesus there were numerous shrines to different gods built in niches in the rock face. Peter, however, declared that Jesus was the son of the living God, the one God in whom he truly believed.

The story of the transfiguration is believed to have taken place on Mount Hermon, north of Galilee. The high slopes are often covered with snow as this picture shows.

Everything Jesus said and did made people ask the question, "Who is Jesus—who can he really be?" Jesus himself was interested to know what people were saying, and asked his disciples what they had heard.

They replied that most people thought he was prophet. Some people thought he was a prophet of old come back to bring God's words to people. Some even thought he was John the Baptist, who had only recently been put to death for his outspoken words about the local king.

"What about you?" he asked them. "Who do you say I am?"
Simon Peter answered, "You are the Messiah, the Son of the living God."
Matthew 16:15–16

Jesus was clearly pleased at Peter's confidence and told him that he would be the rock on which the community of followers would be built. Jesus did not want his disciples to go around telling others that Jesus was the Messiah, the Christ. However, he did begin to talk more and more about the consequences of being the Messiah: he was going to run up against his enemies and be put to death for his message.

The transfiguration

Not long after Jesus asked his disciples who they thought he was, three of them had a chance to see something very special. Jesus went with Peter, James, and John to the top of a high mountain. As the disciples looked at Jesus, they saw a change come over him. His face shone like the sun and his clothes became dazzling white. Two of the

Jesus' disciples were amazed at the heavenly vision of the Transfiguration.

greatest prophets of their people appeared—Moses, the lawgiver, and Elijah, who had stood up for the faith in the time of a cruel and wicked king—and Jesus talked to them.

While he was talking, a shining cloud came over them, and a voice from the cloud said, "This is my own dear Son, with whom I am pleased— listen to him!"

Matthew 17:5

Once again, Jesus told the disciples who saw and heard all this not to say anything until after his death.

✝ The keys of the kingdom

Not only did Jesus call Peter to be the rock and foundation of the church, he also said that he was going to give him the keys to the kingdom of heaven. As a result of these words, it has become traditional in Christian art to depict Peter with elaborate keys.

Peter is also popularly thought of as the gatekeeper of heaven itself—the one who decides whether or not people will be let in. The idea that heaven has pearly gates comes from another part of the Bible: the book of Revelation (written after the time of Jesus) describes the heavenly city as having twelve gates, each made from a single pearl.

A statue of Peter, showing him holding the keys to the kingdom of heaven.

✠ Jesus the light

This picture of Jesus by the British artist Holman Hunt is called *The Light of the World*. It is so well known it has influenced many people's ideas of what Jesus may have looked like.

Jesus also gave his own answers to the question about who he really was. In the Gospel of John are several sayings, all beginning "I am," in which Jesus tries to give a picture of who he is.

The bread of life

On one occasion, Jesus took just a few loaves and fishes and, by a miracle, fed five thousand people. The following day, the people came looking for Jesus. He knew they were eager to see if he could provide more free food. Jesus warned them not to be hungry for food, but for the "bread from heaven" that would satisfy all their deepest longings forever. They asked for this bread, and Jesus gave this answer:

Loaves of bread in the time of Jesus were usually flat like these.

"I am the bread of life," Jesus told them. "Those who come to me will never be hungry; those who believe in me will never be thirsty."
John 6:35

The light of the world

One day, Jesus was talking to the Pharisees. These religious people knew every detail of their laws— the laws God had given Moses—and they knew the Scriptures that described the Law as a light to guide people and show them the way to go. However, Jesus said this to them:

"I am the light of the world," he said. "Whoever follows me will have the light of life and will never walk in darkness."
John 8:12

A typical oil lamp from the time of Jesus.

The good shepherd

Jesus also spoke about his being like a shepherd, leading people as a shepherd leads a flock of sheep and takes care of them.

In his day, sheep were gathered into sheepfolds at night. A sheepfold was a little enclosure made with low stone walls, with just one small entrance. The shepherd himself would lie down in the entrance to keep the sheep in and all danger out. That was what Jesus was talking about when he said, "I am the gate for the sheep."

He also said, "I am the good shepherd." Unlike a hired worker, a good shepherd would stay with his flock even if he had to die to save them.

The resurrection and the life

Just before Jesus raised his friend Lazarus from the dead he made this astonishing promise:

> *"I am the resurrection and the life. Those who believe in me will live, even though they die; and those who live and believe in me will never die."*
>
> **John 11:25–26**

The way to God

As Jesus began to warn his disciples more and more about his death, he told them not to worry. When he died, he was simply going to God to prepare a place for them close to God. "You know the way to God," he told them. They were puzzled by this. So he answered:

> *"I am the way, the truth, and the life; no one goes to the Father except by me."*
>
> **John 14:6**

The vine

Grapevines were a common sight on the hillsides in the land of Jesus. Jesus said:

> *"I am the real vine, and my Father is the gardener. He breaks off every branch in me that does not bear fruit, and he prunes every branch that does bear fruit, so that it will be clean and bear more fruit. . . . I am the vine, and you are the branches. Those who remain in me, and I in them, will bear much fruit. . . . My Father's glory is shown by your bearing much fruit; and in this way you become my disciples. I love you just as the Father loves me; remain in my love. If you obey my commands, you will remain in my love, just as I have obeyed my Father's commands and remain in his love."*
>
> **John 15:1–10**

This reconstructed sheepfold consists of a circular enclosure made with a low stone wall. The top of the wall is covered in spiky thorn branches to help keep wild animals out. There is a wooden gate, but typically the shepherd would have kept watch in the gateway.

Below this fruitful vine are the dry branches that were pruned out at the beginning of the growing season—a perfect picture of Jesus' words that his followers needed to be grafted onto him, the true vine, if they were to be fruitful in good deeds.

37 The Beginning of the End

Look It Up

Jesus rides into Jerusalem:
Mark 11, also Matthew 21, Luke 19, John 12

Different versions

In Matthew, Mark, and Luke, it seems that the great welcome described in this page happens when Jesus makes a special trip to Jerusalem from Galilee. John, however, talks of Jesus having been in Jerusalem for some time teaching the people in and around the Temple.

Differences such as these make some people wonder if the accounts are simply made up. However, many other people think that the differences between the accounts show something else: the writers were so confident of the overall truth of what they were saying they did not have to conspire to make their stories agree in every detail. They simply took the stories they knew and wove them into a story that helped their readers understand more about Jesus.

Jesus was a preacher and teacher for about three years. It was spring: the time of the yearly Passover festival. Jesus told his disciples that they would go to Jerusalem and join the throngs of pilgrims there.

Jesus knew this was dangerous. He warned his disciples several times that he was going to be arrested by the religious leaders and condemned to death. He also said that he would rise again, but the disciples did not understand what he was talking about.

As they approached Jerusalem, Jesus sent two of his disciples on ahead. He gave them instructions about where they would find a donkey, for he wanted to ride into Jerusalem.

As Jesus and his disciples got nearer the city, the crowds who were traveling there noticed him. Some must have remembered the old Scriptures of their people and the prophecy in the book of Zechariah: God had promised to send them a king who would ride to Jerusalem on a donkey. People began to shout:

Noisy crowds welcomed Jesus as a king.

"God bless him who comes in the name of the Lord! God bless the coming kingdom of King David, our father! Praise God!"
Mark 11:9–10

To show their respect, they began to throw their cloaks on the ground for the donkey to walk on, and they cut palm branches and waved them.

It was a turning point. Clearly, there were lots of people who believed Jesus was God's chosen king: the Messiah, the Christ. What was going to happen next?

✞ Palm Sunday

The events leading up to Jesus' death and resurrection are remembered every year in Christian churches. Jesus' riding into Jerusalem is remembered on the Sunday before Easter Sunday—on what is called Palm Sunday. One tradition is for the people to walk in procession around their local area singing traditional hymns.

A Palm Sunday procession in the Cook Islands.

How many donkeys?

Matthew's account of Jesus riding to Jerusalem says there were two donkeys—a mother and her colt. The writer says:

This happened in order to make come true what the prophet had said:
"Tell the city of Zion, Look, your king is coming to you!
He is humble and rides on a donkey and on a colt, the foal of a donkey."
Matthew 21:4–5

Throughout his Gospel, Matthew is keen to point out that in Jesus the old prophesies are coming true.

38  Jesus and the Temple

Jesus, the real Temple

This story of Jesus clearing out the Temple is in all four Gospels. In Matthew, Mark, and Luke it happens very soon after Jesus has been given a hero's welcome in a palm-waving procession. In John's Gospel it is one of the events at the beginning of Jesus' ministry.

John also includes this declaration Jesus makes to the Temple authorities:

"Tear down this Temple, and in three days I will build it again."

"Are you going to build it again in three days?" they asked him. "It has taken forty-six years to build this Temple!"

But the temple Jesus was speaking about was his body. So when he was raised from death, his disciples remembered that he had said this.

John 2:19–22

The Temple in Jerusalem was the focus of the Passover celebrations. Jesus went to the Temple. The huge courtyard was crowded: market traders had set up stalls and were selling things that pilgrims needed for the festival. They had to change their everyday money into Temple money in order to pay the Temple tax. They needed to buy animals to offer as sacrifices—cattle, sheep, and pigeons.

Jesus did not like what he saw. He began to drive the traders out, overturning the tables and the stools.

"It is written in the Scriptures that God said, 'My Temple will be called a house of prayer.' But you are making it a hideout for thieves!"
Matthew 21:13

The chief priests were very angry at what Jesus had done.

Jesus caused uproar in the Temple courtyard.

Parable of tenants in the vineyard

Jesus told the following parable.

There was once a man who built a vineyard, with a fence around it, a watchtower in the corner, and a winepress. Then he went on a journey and let the vineyard to tenants. When the harvest time came, he sent a servant to collect his share.

The tenants beat him and sent him away with nothing.

The owner sent another servant, and the same thing happened. He sent more servants. Some were beaten; others were killed.

In the end, the man sent his son. "I'm sure they will respect my son," he said.

But when the tenants saw the son, they saw their chance. "Let's kill him," they agreed, "then the vineyard will be ours." So they did.

"What do you think will happen next?" Jesus asked his listeners. "The owner will come and kill those murderers and hand the vineyard on to others."

The religious leaders were furious. They recognized that the parable was against them. The owner was meant to be God, the servants were the prophets and the tenants were themselves. In his story, Jesus was hinting that they had not taken care of the things that God had wanted them to, and that they were failing to recognize that Jesus was God's son.

The tenants in the vineyard of Jesus' story had forgotten that it belonged to someone else and had begun to treat it as their home.

The poor widow

As Jesus sat near the Temple, he watched people coming to bring their offerings. Many rich people came and gave a lot. Then a poor widow came along and dropped in two copper coins, worth only a little. "This woman has given more than the others," he said to his disciples, "because she has given all she had."

Jesus was angry that the teachers of the Law, who loved to flaunt how religious they were, didn't take proper care of the poor.

The thirteen collecting boxes in the Temple were known as shofarot: the word *shofar* means trumpet, and it seems the boxes had a trumpet shaped opening. This design made it easy for donors to put money in but impossible for the sly to dip their hands in and take money out.

Look It Up

Judas:
Matthew 26, Mark 14, Luke 22

The plot against Jesus:
John 11, also Matthew 26, Mark 14, Luke 22

Jesus: The anointed one:
Matthew 26, also Mark 14, John 12

Judas

The religious leaders had a major problem trying to work out how to arrest Jesus. When he was surrounded by crowds, they could never come and take him away because the people would riot. When he went off with his disciples, they didn't know where to find him.

Their chance came when one of Jesus' disciples, Judas Iscariot, came to them to talk about betraying Jesus. The priests gave him thirty pieces of silver in return for information about where to find Jesus when he was alone. Judas began to look for a good opportunity to tip them off.

Judas secretly agreed to betray Jesus to the religious leaders.

The things Jesus did and said won him many followers. However, the religious leaders—the teachers of the Law and the Temple priests—were getting more and more angry with him: his interpretation of the Law, his miracles, and his popularity all offended them.

John, in his Gospel, gives another reason why they were anxious to get rid of Jesus. Because Jesus could work miracles, the crowds who followed him were treating him as a local hero. The Romans who ruled the land could easily mistake Jesus for a rebel leader.

"If we let Jesus go on this way," they said, "everyone will believe in him, and the Roman authorities will take action and destroy our Temple and our nation!"

They argued that it was better for everyone to hand Jesus over, letting him die instead of having the whole nation destroyed.

Rebelling against the Romans

The Jewish authorities were quite right to be anxious about the Romans: they were happy to allow the people they ruled quite a lot of freedom about how they lived and the religion they followed as long as they did not challenge their authority. If the Romans felt their right to rule was being challenged they could be merciless.

In fact, the Jews did rebel against the Romans not long after the time of Jesus, around 70 CE. In the bitter fighting, the Romans overran the Temple in Jerusalem, destroying the building and taking the treasures away. On the next page, you can read about the last stand the Jews made against the Romans at Masada.

The Roman emperor whose armies defeated the Jews was called Titus, and a triumphal arch was built to honor him in Rome. It shows men carrying away treasures from the Temple in Jerusalem, including ceremonial trumpets and the seven-branched golden lampstand.

This wall is all that remains of the Jewish Temple today. It was not part of the magnificent building—simply a retaining wall for the huge platform on which the Temple stood. Even so, it is a special place for Jews, who come from all over the world to pray here.

Jesus: The anointed one

Around the same time that the priests were plotting to get rid of Jesus, something very important happened. While Jesus was eating in the house of one of his friends, a woman came in with a jar of the finest perfume and poured it over him. Some of the people who saw this—including Judas—were angry at the waste. "It could have been sold, and the money given to the poor," they said.

Jesus told them to leave her alone. "You will always have poor people in this world, and if you want to give money to help them, you can do so," he explained. He accepted her generosity and took it as a sign of anointing. An anointing ceremony was done to mark out the person who was going to be the nation's king, making them the "messiah" or anointed one (or in Greek, "Christ"). But it was also done to a person who had died, as part of getting the body ready for burial. Jesus knew that he was going to die.

Anointing

The ancient ceremony of anointing involved pouring oil over the head of the chosen person, possibly from a jar such as this one. It was a way of showing that God's favor was being poured over the person.

The first kings of the Jewish people had been anointed by a prophet named Samuel: Saul was the first king and David the second.

40  Jesus' Final Warnings

Jesus knew that his disagreements with the religious leaders were coming to a crisis point. According to Matthew, Mark, and Luke, he gave his disciples some serious warnings about wars and disasters ahead—and, indeed, the end of the world as we know it.

Be ready

Jesus warned his disciples that no one except God knew when these events would take place. They must stay on watch for God to make them happen, like servants waiting for their master to come. He also told this story:

"At that time the Kingdom of heaven will be like this. Once there were ten young women who took their oil lamps and went out to meet the bridegroom. Five of them were foolish, and the other five were wise.

The foolish ones took their lamps but did not take any extra oil with them, while the wise ones took containers full of oil for their lamps. The bridegroom was late in coming, so they began to nod and fall asleep.

"It was already midnight when the cry rang out, 'Here is the bridegroom! Come and meet him!' The ten young women woke up and trimmed their lamps. Then the foolish ones said to the wise ones, 'Let us have some of your oil, because our lamps are going out.' 'No, indeed,' the wise ones answered, 'there is not enough for you and for us. Go to the shop and buy some for yourselves.'

Five bridesmaids are ready to greet the bridegroom on his arrival.

Look It Up

The end times:
Matthew 24, Mark 13, Luke 12, 17, 21

Be ready:
Matthew 25

The final judgment:
Matthew 25

The clifftop fortress of Masada was the last Jewish stronghold in their rebellion against the Romans.

The end times

Jesus' disciples were puzzled by some of the warnings Jesus gave about the troubles ahead. Years later, they may have linked the warnings to a major war between Jewish rebels and the Romans. In those troubles, the Temple was destroyed and the Jews scattered over the empire.

A handful of Jewish rebels held out for a long time in the hilltop fort of Masada, near the Dead Sea. They were trapped as, over many weeks, the besieging army built an earth ramp up the steep rocky sides of the fortress and stormed it. However, the Romans found that nearly all the rebels had committed suicide—they preferred death to defeat.

84

"So the foolish ones went off to buy some oil; and while they were gone, the bridegroom arrived. The five who were ready went in with him to the wedding feast, and the door was closed.

"Later the others arrived. 'Sir, sir! Let us in!' they cried out. 'Certainly not! I don't know you,' the bridegroom answered."

And Jesus concluded, "Watch out, then, because you do not know the day or the hour."

Matthew 25:1–13

Five bridesmaids have forgotten to bring enough oil for their lamps so they miss the celebration.

The final judgment

Jesus warned that there would be a final judgment:

"When the Son of Man comes as King and all the angels with him, he will sit on his royal throne, and the people of all the nations will be gathered before him. Then he will divide them into two groups, just as a shepherd separates the sheep from the goats."

Matthew 25:31–32

Jesus went on to say how the righteous will be welcomed into the kingdom for their good deeds toward the king, and they will answer:

"'When, Lord, did we ever see you hungry and feed you, or thirsty and give you a drink? When did we ever see you a stranger and welcome you in our homes, or naked and clothe you? When did we ever see you sick or in prison, and visit you?' The King will reply, 'I tell you, whenever you did this for one of the least important of these members of mine, you did it for me!'"

Matthew 25:37–40

Meanwhile, the others will be sent away to a miserable end.

✛ The end is nigh

Some Christians today study the sayings of Jesus anxiously, looking for hints of what they might mean about the end of the world. However, Jesus made it clear that the end of all things is in the hand of God alone, and the duty of Christians is to follow the teachings of Jesus without fail, so that at the end they will still be busy doing good, as Jesus taught.

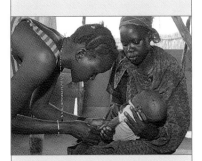

A Christian doctor helps to heal the sick.

Christian relief workers are concerned to provide food, clothing, and shelter for the very poor.

41 Jesus and the Passover Meal

Look It Up

Jesus and the Passover meal:
Mark 14, also Matthew 26, Luke 22, John 13

The old covenant and the new:
Luke 22, also Matthew 26, Mark 14, 1 Corinthians 11

Feasting

It was a Roman custom for people to recline on couches around a low table for feasting. Even though the Passover meal was a Jewish festival, it is likely that Jesus and his disciples would have done the same.

Jesus had come to Jerusalem with his disciples to celebrate the festival of Passover. In spite of the danger from his enemies, he asked his disciples to get everything ready for the meal. He himself must have made some plans, for he told them to go into the city where someone carrying a water jar would meet them. They were to follow the man to a house, and then ask the owner to show them the room that he was going to lend to Jesus. The owner showed them an upstairs room, and the disciples prepared the festival meal, as Jesus had instructed.

The old covenant and the new

The Passover meal was very important. It reminded the Jewish people of the time of the first Passover, when God had enabled Moses to lead the people out of Egypt, where they had been slaves. After their escape, God made a promise to the people: they must keep God's laws, and God would take them to a land which they could make their home. This promise was also called a covenant. At the meal, Jesus said something very special about a new covenant:

Judas slipped away from the meal to betray Jesus.

86

He took a piece of bread, gave thanks to God, broke it, and gave it to them, saying, "This is my body, which is given for you. Do this in memory of me." In the same way, he gave them the cup after the supper, saying, "This cup is God's new covenant sealed with my blood, which is poured out for you."

Luke 22:19–20

As Jesus knew he would, Judas took his moment to go and betray Jesus to the people who wanted to arrest him when he was alone. Other disciples began arguing about which of them was going to be the most important—and Jesus had to tell them that among his followers, the greatest must be like a servant to the least, as he himself was.

Jesus also knew that even loyal Peter was going to deny knowing him in the troubles that lay ahead.

Then, as they had done before, Jesus and his followers went out of the city to the nearby Mount of Olives.

This painting from the catacombs in Rome shows Christians sharing a meal together as Jesus had commanded. In the early days of the faith, Christianity was illegal, and believers met secretly in this network of tunnels in Rome.

✠ Bread and wine

The ceremony of sharing bread and wine as Jesus had commanded at his last supper with his disciples quickly became an important one for Jesus' followers. A few years later, one of the first Christian leaders, Paul, wrote a letter to the believers in Corinth reminding them to conduct the ceremony in the right way.

Through the history of the Christian church, believers have always been concerned to treat the ceremony with the greatest respect.

Jesus and his disciples celebrated a last supper together.

When Christians today share these elements, they reflect on what Jesus said about his body and his blood.

42 The Last Supper: John's Account

John's story of the last supper is rather different from that of the other Gospel writers. It says that the meal was the one before the Passover festival, when Jesus knew that the time had come for him to leave this world and return to God.

At the supper, he got up from the table and got ready to wash his disciples' feet, as a servant would in those days. After he had done so, he explained what he had done:

"You call me Teacher and Lord, and it is right that you do so, because that is what I am. I, your Lord and Teacher, have just washed your feet. . . . I have set an example for you, so that you will do just what I have done for you. I am telling you the truth: no slaves are greater than their master, and no messengers are never greater than the one who sent them."
John 13:13–16

But by now Jesus was very upset, for he knew that one of his disciples was going to betray him. Peter wanted to know who, and Jesus said he would pass some bread to the one who had turned against him: he passed it to Judas. "Be quick about what you are doing," said Jesus as Judas hurried away, although the others did not understand where he was going.

Jesus washed Peter's feet. He wanted to show his followers what it meant to serve one another.

Look It Up

The last supper:
John 13–14

A servant's job

It was the custom in Jesus' day for guests to be welcomed into a house with the chance to wash their feet. This was because people wore sandals in the hot climate, and their feet quickly became dirty as they walked along the dusty paths and tracks. At the very least, a guest would expect to be given a bowl of water in which to wash his own feet. However, it was more usual that the job would be done by a servant. This clay bath is the kind of bowl that might have been used.

The new commandment

After Judas had gone, Jesus gave his faithful disciples a new commandment:

"My children, I shall not be with you very much longer. You will look for me; but I tell you now what I told the Jewish authorities, 'You cannot go where I am going.' And now I give you a new commandment: love one another. As I have loved you, so you must love one another. If you have love for one another, then everyone will know that you are my disciples."

John 13:33–35

Jesus and Peter

Peter did not fully understand what Jesus was saying and asked him to explain where he was going. Jesus simply replied that Peter could not follow him there yet.

"Lord, why can't I follow you now?" asked Peter. "I am ready to die for you!"

Jesus answered, "Are you really ready to die for me? I am telling you the truth: before the rooster crows you will say three times that you do not know me."

John 13:37–38

The Holy Spirit

Jesus then spoke to the disciples, reassuring them that all would be well, in spite of the terrible things that were about to happen, in spite of the fact that it was time for him to leave the world and go back to his Father in heaven.

"If you love me, you will obey my commandments. I will ask the Father, and he will give you another Helper, who will stay with you forever. He is the Spirit who reveals the truth about God."

John 14:15–17

Then, before leaving the house, Jesus prayed that God would keep his disciples safe.

✛ Foot washing

John's Gospel does not mention the sharing of bread and wine but only the foot washing. A ceremony of foot washing does take place in many churches once a year, on the evening before the day that Jesus' crucifixion is remembered. This day is sometimes known as Maundy Thursday.

A few groups of Christians include foot washing more often in the life of the church. Among them are the Anabaptist groups of North America. The ceremony reminds them that they are to serve one another and not to think that some people in the church are more important than others.

The archbishop of Canterbury is the head of the Anglican church worldwide. When he revived the ceremony of foot washing on the Thursday of Holy Week, he deliberately chose to wash the feet not only of men—as had become the custom in many churches—but of women as well.

43 Jesus Is Arrested

It was night in Jerusalem. Jesus had shared a special meal with his friends. He had warned them of hard times ahead. Judas had gone out on his own.

Then, as many times before, Jesus and eleven disciples went out of the city, across the Kidron Brook, to an olive grove on the next hill, the Mount of Olives.

Look It Up

Jesus prays alone:
Mark 14, also Matthew 26, Luke 22

The betrayal:
Luke 22, also Matthew 26, Mark 14, John 18

Peter's denial:
Matthew 26, Mark 14, Luke 22, John 18

An olive grove.

The Mount of Olives

The place where Jesus was betrayed was on a hill just outside Jerusalem—directly opposite the Temple, which was built on top of the so-called Mount Zion.

The name, "the Mount of Olives," suggests that in the time of Jesus its slopes were covered with olive groves. The dense, bushy trees would have shut out any light in the night-time sky, and the shadows would have hidden Jesus and his disciples from any enemies —if only they had not been led to him.

Soldiers came to arrest Jesus and take him to the religious authorities.

Jesus prays alone

Matthew, Mark, and Luke say that in the olive grove, the Garden of Gethsemane, Jesus wanted to pray. He took Peter, James, and John with him and asked them to stay awake with him. Then he went further off on his own.

His prayer was full of anguish:

"Father," he prayed, "my Father! All things are possible for you. Take this cup of suffering away from me. Yet not what I want, but what you want."

Mark 14:36

When Jesus returned to the three, he found they had fallen asleep and was sad that they could not watch with him. He went to pray a second time, and when he returned they had fallen asleep again. Now they felt very embarrassed. A third time it happened. Jesus woke them: he could see his betrayer.

The betrayal

Judas arrived, leading a band of soldiers that the religious leaders had provided for him. He went up to Jesus and greeted him as was the custom, with a kiss. The armed men arrested Jesus. There was a scuffle. One of the high priest's servants had his ear cut off, but Jesus healed him and allowed himself to be led away.

Peter's denial

All the disciples except Peter ran away. He followed as Jesus was taken to the council of priests, elders, and teachers of the Law at the high priest's house. Peter sat in the courtyard, warming himself by the fire.

Then a servant girl came by. "You were with Jesus of Nazareth, weren't you?" she said.

Peter denied it. Then he heard her saying the same to other people in the courtyard, and again he denied it. Then one of the others came and said the same. "Your accent shows you're from Galilee, like Jesus," he said. A third time Peter denied it.

Then the cock crowed. It was nearly dawn. Suddenly, Peter remembered that Jesus had warned this would happen, and he wept.

Jesus looks at Peter in this nineteenth-century painting.

✟ The look

Luke gives an extra detail in the story of Peter denying that he knows Jesus. On the third denial, he says that Jesus turned around and was able to look directly at Peter. It was this look that reminded Peter of his boast the evening before that he would never do such a thing.

The incident is remembered in numerous works of art. Christians feel they themselves often let Jesus down, just as Peter did. A picture of the look Jesus gave is a reminder to them to be more faithful.

44  Jesus on Trial

Look It Up

Jesus on trial:
Matthew 26, Mark 14, Luke 22, John 18

Trial by night

Jewish law in the time of Jesus forbade trials taking place at night—and one practical reason for such a law is that people who are lacking sleep may not make good judgments. The illegal time of the trial and the fact that witnesses had to be paid are mentioned in the Gospels as evidence that Jesus' trial before the Jewish authorities was completely unfair.

These steps in Jerusalem are believed to lead from the house of the high priest where Jesus was tried. Many Christian pilgrims believe that Jesus would have been hustled down these steps.

It was the middle of the night. Jesus looked at a sea of faces: the elders and the teachers of the Law who hated him. They wanted to find a reason to get rid of him.

One by one people were asked to speak, but even though they told lies, there was no evidence of Jesus having done wrong. In the end, the trial hinged on one question they asked Jesus: "Are you the Messiah, the Son of God?"

Here are the answers that the Gospel writers say he gave.

Matthew

"So you say. But I tell all of you: from this time on you will see the Son of Man sitting on the right side of the Almighty and coming on the clouds of heaven!"
Matthew 26:64

Mark

"I am," answered Jesus, "and you will all see the Son of Man seated at the right side of the Almighty and coming with the clouds of heaven!"
Mark 14:62

Luke

"If I tell you, you will not believe me; and if I ask you a question, you will not answer. But from now on the Son of Man will be seated at the right side of Almighty God."
They all said, "Are you, then, the Son of God?"
He answered them, "You say that I am."
Luke 22:67–70

John

John's Gospel describes the trial rather differently. The high priest questioned Jesus about his teaching and Jesus answered:

"I have always spoken publicly to everyone; all my teaching was done in the synagogues and in the Temple, where all the people come together. I have never said anything in secret. Why, then, do you question me? Question the people who heard me. Ask them what I told them—they know what I said."
John 18:20–21

Whatever was said, Jesus' accusers had already made up their minds: Jesus was trouble. In the trial they claimed he was making people believe he was someone special to God when he wasn't. They believed this was an insult to God: Jesus was committing the sin of blasphemy. However, a key reason for their wanting to get rid of Jesus was that they feared he would cause such a stir that the Romans would clamp down on the whole nation.

Only the Roman authorities were allowed to issue the death penalty, so they took Jesus to the governor, Pontius Pilate.

Witnesses brought their accusations against Jesus to the high priest and the rest of the Jewish council.

The high priest

Jesus' nighttime trial was held in the house of the high priest, whose name was Caiaphas. In the time of Jesus, the high priest was chosen by the Romans: they wanted the person in this influential position to be someone who would support their rule. He was almost certainly better known for his political cunning than his godliness!

The high priest's breastplate bore twelve jewels—one for each of the tribes of Israel—as a reminder of the belief that they were dear to God's heart.

The high priest wore a ceremonial turban. According to the instructions given in the time of Moses, the gold ornament was to be engraved with the words "Dedicated to the Lord."

45 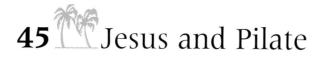 Jesus and Pilate

Jesus and the Romans

The Gospels do not have much to say about Jesus and the Romans, apart from one story when he healed the servant of a Roman soldier because of the man's unquestioning faith.

However, a few days before the trial, the Pharisees tried to trap Jesus into saying something about the Romans that would condemn him.

They asked him if it was right to pay taxes to the emperor.

Jesus replied:

"Why are you trying to trap me? Bring a silver coin, and let me see it."
They brought him one, and he asked,
"Whose face and name are these?"

"The Emperor's," they answered.
So Jesus said, "Well, then, pay to the Emperor what belongs to the Emperor, and pay to God what belongs to God."

Mark 12:15–17

The Roman governor, Pontius Pilate, had no real interest in Jesus. His job was to make sure the country obeyed Roman law and that there was no uprising against the emperor. When the religious leaders brought him Jesus on a charge of blasphemy, he was puzzled. He neither understood nor cared about their religious law.

Pilate questioned Jesus and couldn't find anything for which to condemn him. Luke says he sent him to the local king of Galilee, Herod, and that didn't lead to any case against him either. Pilate would have been happy to let him go with just a whipping, but the religious leaders persisted in seeking the death penalty. So Pilate tried again.

Barabbas was a rebel fighter and a murderer.

At every Passover Festival Pilate was in the habit of setting free any one prisoner the people asked for. At that time a man named Barabbas was in prison with the rebels who had committed murder in the riot. When the crowd gathered and began to ask Pilate for the usual favor, he asked them, "Do you want me to set free for you the king of the Jews?" He knew very well that the chief priests had handed Jesus over to him because they were jealous.

But the chief priests stirred up the crowd to ask, instead, for Pilate to set Barabbas free for them. Pilate spoke again to the crowd, "What, then, do you want me to do with the one you call the king of the Jews?"

They shouted back, "Crucify him!"

"But what crime has he committed?" Pilate asked.

They shouted all the louder, "Crucify him!"

Pilate wanted to please the crowd, so he set Barabbas free for them. Then he had Jesus whipped and handed him over to be crucified.

Mark 15:6–15

According to Matthew, Pilate's wife sent a message warning him to have nothing to do with Jesus' execution.

✠ Here is the man

According to John's Gospel, Pilate sent Jesus to be whipped by his soldiers before he had decided whether or not to condemn him to death. The soldiers dressed him in a robe of royal hue and crowned him with thorns. Jesus was dressed like this when Pilate brought him to the crowd to ask for their views on how to punish him. The words he used have been translated in Latin as "Ecce homo" and in older English translations as "Behold the man." Numerous works of art have depicted this moment.

Jesus' kingdom

Jesus' enemies told Pilate he was claiming to be the king of the Jews, which would make him look like a rebel. When Pilate asked Jesus if that was true, he gave this reply:

"My kingdom does not belong to this world; if my kingdom belonged to this world, my followers would fight to keep me from being handed over to the Jewish authorities. No, my kingdom does not belong here!"

So Pilate asked him, "Are you a king, then?"

Jesus answered, "You say that I am a king. I was born and came into the world for this one purpose, to speak about the truth. Whoever belongs to the truth listens to me."

John 18:36–37

According to Matthew, Pilate washed his hands in public. It was to show that he was clean of any responsibility for the death of Jesus.

Pilate did not fully understand the answer, but he still did not think that Jesus deserved death.

Pontius Pilate

S TIBERIEVM
PONTIVSPILATVS
PRAEFECTVSIVD...E

The stone slab above was found in Caesarea, on the coast of the land where Jesus lived. Below it are the letters that are still visible and some that have been destroyed. They reveal that Pilate built a shrine to the emperor Tiberius—a Tiberieum—when he was the prefect of the area. This stone is further evidence that the story of Jesus belongs to real history.

Judas

When Judas found out that Jesus had been condemned, he took the money he had been paid back to the priests and said he had sinned by betraying an innocent man. The priests didn't care. Matthew says that Judas flung down the money and went and hanged himself. Luke says that he bought a field and fell to his death there.

Look It Up

The road to the cross:
Mark 15, John 19, also Matthew 27, Luke 23

Carrying the cross:
Luke 23, also Matthew 27, Mark 15

The outcrops of rock on this hill near old Jerusalem look like a skull, and some people think this place may be Golgotha.

The place of crucifixion

No one knows for sure where Jesus was crucified. The Gospels say that it was outside the city, near a road, and easy to see from a distance—so perhaps on a hill. The place was called Golgotha—the Place of the Skull.

Some modern translations of the Bible and many hymns say that Jesus was crucified at Calvary. This word comes from the Latin word for a skull.

"King of the Jews?" The soldiers had learned to be bullies, and the charge against Jesus was their opening. They dressed him in a purple robe of the same color that the emperor wore as a sign of his rank. They made a crown of thorns and pushed it hard onto his head. They gave him a stick as a symbol of his power. Then they mocked him.

The soldiers led Jesus out of the Roman fortress of Antonia to be crucified.

This picture shows what the route to the cross may have looked like in Jesus' day.

Carrying the cross

Next, the soldiers dressed Jesus in his own clothes and gave him the wood for his cross to carry. On the way to the place of execution, they met a man named Simon who was coming from a place called Cyrene to Jerusalem. The soldiers decided to make him carry the wood.

Luke says that a large crowd of people followed Jesus, including some women who were weeping for him. Jesus turned and told them not to weep for him but for themselves, for troubled times lay ahead.

The soldiers led Jesus to a place of execution outside the city walls—somewhere called the Place of the Skull, or, in Hebrew, Golgotha.

This church picture shows one of the stations of the cross—where Simon of Cyrene is ordered to help carry the cross.

Jesus was led through the streets of Jerusalem to a place outside the city wall.

✝ Stations of the Cross

Every Friday in Jerusalem, Christians still walk the Way of the Cross—a traditional route through the city. They stop at different points along the way to remember events from the Gospels and other old traditions of what happened on Jesus' walk to his crucifixion.

These stopping points are called the "Stations of the Cross." Traditionally there are fourteen, and a fifteenth about Jesus' resurrection. Many churches have fifteen pictures around the walls for Christians to "walk with Jesus."

Some countries have the tradition of arranging the Stations of the Cross up a hill—a Calvary. Pilgrims walk up to the cross at the top.

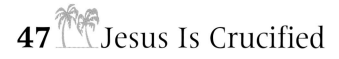

The soldiers gambled to win Jesus' tunic. Here is a Roman gaming board found on a pavement in Jerusalem.

When they reached the place of execution, the soldiers offered Jesus a drugged drink to dull the pain, but he refused it. They went ahead and crucified Jesus, nailing him to a cross of wood.

Then the four soldiers divided his possessions. John says that they didn't want to tear Jesus' tunic, which was woven in one piece. Instead, they played dice to find out who would win it.

The two thieves

Two criminals were also crucified that day, one on the left of Jesus and one on the right. Luke says that one of them joined in with the crowds who were jeering at Jesus, saying that if he was the Messiah he should prove it and save both himself and them.

The other one, however, rebuked him, saying, "Don't you fear God? You received the same sentence he did. Ours, however, is only right, because we are getting what we deserve for what we did; but he has done no wrong."

And he said to Jesus, "Remember me, Jesus, when you come as King!"

Jesus said to him, "I promise you that today you will be in Paradise with me."

Luke 23:40–43

The Gospels each tell a story of what Jesus said as he hung on the cross.

A reconstruction of a first-century cross.

✠ INRI

People who were crucified had a placard announcing their crime nailed to their cross. Pilate wrote the placard for Jesus. It read, "Jesus of Nazareth, the king of the Jews." The chief priests wanted him to change it to say, "This man said, 'I am the king of the Jews,'" but Pilate said that what he had written was the way it would stay.

The words of the Latin version begin with the letters INRI, which you will see in many pictures of the crucifixion.

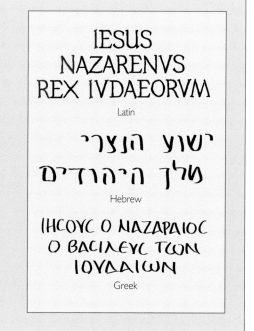

IESUS NAZARENVS REX IVDAEORVM
Latin

ישוע הנצרי
מלך היהודים
Hebrew

IHCOYC O NAZAPAIOC O BACIΛEYC TⲰN IOYΔAIⲰN
Greek

Forgiveness and trust

Luke tells us that Jesus said a prayer for his executioners.

"Forgive them, Father! They don't know what they are doing."
Luke 23:34

As Jesus grew weaker, the sky went dark for three hours. Then something happened to tear the curtain in the Temple that shrouded the Holy Place. Jesus cried out:

"Father! In your hands I place my spirit." *He said this and died.*
Luke 23:46

Mark and Matthew recalled that one of the soldiers who saw Jesus die was moved to say that Jesus really was the Son of God.

Despair

Mark says that after the three long hours of darkness Jesus cried out:

"Eloi, Eloi, lema sabachthani?"
Mark 15:34

It means, "My God, my God, why did you abandon me?" Someone came to offer him a drink from a wine-soaked sponge, but Jesus died.

Matthew tells the same story and says that the earth shook, graves were torn open, and dead people were seen walking into Jerusalem.

Concern for others

John says that Jesus saw his mother, Mary, and John, "the disciple he loved," at the foot of the cross. He said to his mother, "He is your son," and to John, "She is your mother." It was a request for John to take care of her. Then he said, "I am thirsty," and was given a drink from a wine-soaked sponge. Finally Jesus said,

"It is finished!" *Then he bowed his head and gave up his spirit.*
John 19:30

When the soldiers came by to check on the state of the condemned men, they had to break the legs of the other two to speed up their dying. Jesus was already dead, but they plunged a spear into his side.

An ornate rood screen in an Anglican church in Cornwall, England.

✝ The rood

Rood" is an old word for cross. In the Middle Ages, many churches were designed with a screen between the part of the church where the people sat and the part where the priest led the worship by the altar. The screen is called the rood screen.

Along the top of a rood screen is a depiction of Jesus on the cross, with his mother, Mary, watching on one side and the disciple John on the other.

The symbolism of the rood screen is that one can only approach God's holiness through what Jesus accomplished by dying on the cross.

48  The Burial of Jesus

Look It Up

The burial of Jesus:
Matthew 27, Mark 15, Luke 23, John 19

✚ The pieta

The pieta is the name given to depictions such as the one shown above of Mary, the mother of Jesus, holding the body of her son. The Gospels do not mention her doing so, although they do say she was at the crucifixion and stayed with the disciples afterwards.

Jesus was crucified on the day before the Jewish Sabbath. It was therefore important that the body be dealt with before the Sabbath day of rest began, at sunset.

A man named Joseph from Arimathea went to ask Pilate for the body. Pilate asked the guard to confirm that the prisoner was dead, and Joseph went to collect the body. He wrapped it in a cloth and had it taken to a tomb. Then he had the huge stone door rolled in place. Joseph had bought the tomb for himself: it was a cave cut out of solid rock and had never been used.

John says that a man named Nicodemus went with Joseph to prepare the body for burial. The other Gospels say that a group of women went. Mark and Matthew name them as Mary Magdalene and another Mary.

The guard at the tomb

According to Matthew, the religious leaders were still worried about what Jesus' followers might do. On the Sabbath itself they went to Pilate and warned him that Jesus had said he would be raised to life; it was important that the body be kept safe so his followers could not start spreading rumors. Pilate gave them a guard to watch the tomb, and they put a seal on the door so it would be obvious if it had been broken.

The garden tomb is a popular place of pilgrimage in Jerusalem.

✦ Where was Jesus buried?

There are two places in Jerusalem where Christian pilgrims go to see a tomb and remember Jesus' burial.

One is known as the Garden Tomb. In the nineteenth century a British army officer named General Gordon suggested that this might be the right place. The tomb consists of a low room cut into the rock, with ledges where a body would have been laid—although now the tomb itself is rather disappointingly shabby, and the entrance is patched with an ugly wall.

More recent research suggests that the tomb is much older than the time of Jesus, and so cannot be the one that Joseph of Arimathea would have had prepared. Nevertheless, because it is so clearly an ancient tomb and because it is surrounded by well-tended and peaceful gardens, it remains a popular place for Christians to visit.

The other is in the Church of the Holy Sepulchre. Not long after the time of Jesus, Jerusalem was destroyed and rebuilt by the Romans. Only in 326 CE, when the emperor Constantine became a Christian, did people set about rediscovering important Christian sites. Local Christians suggested where to dig, and a tomb was discovered. Much of the stone was cut away to create a shrine around it. Over the centuries the site was damaged by earthquake, fire, and war, but pilgrims still came and, over many years, a church was built.

All the evidence gathered to this day suggests that this site could well be the right place.

This elaborate monument houses the traditional tomb of Christ in the Church of the Holy Sepulchre.

✦ Holy Week

In many branches of the Christian church, the week beginning on Palm Sunday is known as Holy Week. In these few days, Jesus' followers discovered that Jesus was not going to make himself a king on earth. Instead, he trusted in God to bring a different kind of victory—the victory of the resurrection!

A crown of thorns—a symbol that Jesus chose the way of suffering.

Joseph of Arimathea

The man who collected Jesus' body from the cross was a member of the Jewish council that had put Jesus on trial. He had disagreed with their verdict, but his opinion was not enough to save Jesus.

Because of his status, the Roman authorities would have respected him when he came to ask for Jesus' body. The fact that he had had a tomb prepared for his own death indicates that he was quite wealthy.

49 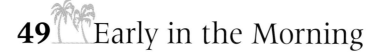 Early in the Morning

The resurrection

The miracle of Jesus' rising from death to new life is known as the resurrection. It is at the heart of the Christian faith. One of the most important people who helped spread the Christian faith not long after the time of Jesus was someone called Paul. He wrote:

If Christ has not been raised from death, then we have nothing to preach and you have nothing to believe. . . .

And if Christ has not been raised, then your faith is a delusion and you are still lost in your sins. . . .

If our hope in Christ is good for this life only and no more, then we deserve more pity than anyone else in all the world.

1 Corinthians 15:14–19

However, Paul then goes on to tell of his complete confidence in the miracle of Jesus' resurrection and his complete faith that God will raise to life all those who die believing in Jesus Christ. He declares that the scripture will come true:

"Death is destroyed; victory is complete!"

1 Corinthians 15:54

Christians believe that just as a seed must fall to the ground if it is to grow, so everyone must die before they can be part of God's kingdom.

The day after the Sabbath, just as dawn was breaking, some women went to the tomb.

The earthquake and the angel

Matthew says that Mary Magdalene and another Mary went to look at the tomb. There was an earthquake, and an angel rolled the stone door open. The soldiers guarding the tomb collapsed as if dead. The angel told the women that Jesus was alive and had gone to Galilee. As the women rushed to tell the disciples, they met Jesus and were overjoyed.

Meanwhile, the guards went and told the religious leaders all that had happened. They were given money to spread the story that Jesus' followers had stolen the body.

The open door and the angel

Mark says that three women went to the tomb— Mary Magdalene, Mary, the mother of James, and Salome. They had spices with which to prepare the body for its burial. They were wondering about how to roll the door open when they saw that the stone had been moved. Inside was a young man dressed in white. He told them Jesus was alive and was going to Galilee. They ran away terrified.

The empty tomb

Luke says that Mary Magdalene, Joanna, and Mary, the mother of James, went to the tomb with burial spices. They found the stone door open and the tomb empty. As they were wondering what this meant, two men in shining clothes came and stood by them.

"Why are you looking among the dead for one who is alive? He is not here; he has been raised."

Luke 24:5–6

The women went and told the disciples. No one believed the story. Peter ran to the tomb and saw the cloths that had been wrapped around the body and nothing else.

The man in the garden

John says that Mary Magdalene went to the tomb early on Sunday morning. She found it open and empty. She hurried to fetch Peter and John, who went in and saw the grave cloths. The disciples went home, but Mary waited by the tomb. When she looked in again she saw two angels dressed in white. They asked her why she was crying. She replied, "They have taken my Lord away, and I do not know where they have put him."

Then she turned around. A man was standing there, and he too asked why she was crying.

She thought he was the gardener, so she said to him, "If you took him away, tell me where you have put him, and I will go and get him."

Jesus said to her, "Mary!"

Then Mary recognized him: Jesus, her beloved teacher.

So Mary went and told the disciples.

Mary Magdalene recognized Jesus.

Look It Up

Doubting Thomas:
John 20

The road to Emmaus:
Luke 24, also Mark 16, Matthew 28

I'm going fishing:
John 21

Three questions:
John 21

✝ Doubting Thomas

Poor Thomas! He was out when the risen Jesus appeared to the other disciples. It is hardly surprising that he found it hard to believe that they had seen Jesus alive when he hadn't. However, because of this he has become known as "Doubting Thomas"—and anyone who is not easily convinced of something is often called a doubting Thomas.

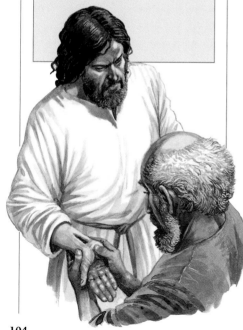

On resurrection day, and for forty days afterward, the disciples saw Jesus, talked with him, and shared meals with him.

The road to Emmaus

On the Sunday morning, two of Jesus' followers were walking from Jerusalem to Emmaus. A man who was going the same way came by and asked what they were talking about. The one named Cleopas explained that everyone was talking about Jesus of Nazareth—the one everyone had hoped would set their people free, who had been executed and who was now rumored to have been seen alive.

The man explained that all that had happened was exactly what the Scriptures had predicted about the Messiah. They were intrigued and asked the man to be their guest that night. As they sat down to eat, the man said the blessing and broke the bread. It was Jesus!

At once, the man disappeared. Cleopas and his companion hurried back to the disciples in Jerusalem.

Luke then says that the two were just telling their news to the disciples when Jesus appeared. He showed them his wounded hands and feet and ate some of the meal to prove he was not a ghost. Mark's Gospel includes a similar story.

John says that ten of the disciples were in a room in Jerusalem together on that Sunday evening. They were overjoyed to see Jesus and excitedly told the news to the eleventh, Thomas, when he returned. Thomas, however, simply could not believe their story.

"Unless I see the scars of the nails in his hands and put my finger on those scars and my hand in his side, I will not believe."
John 20:25

A week went by. Once again they were all together and the room was safely locked. Then Jesus appeared and asked Thomas to touch him.

Thomas answered him, "My Lord and my God!"
Jesus said to him, "Do you believe because you see me? How happy are those who believe without seeing me!"
John 20:28–29

When Thomas saw Jesus' wounds, he believed that Jesus must have risen from the dead.

Matthew's Gospel simply states that the risen Jesus met with his eleven disciples on a hill in Galilee. John, however, tells another story about Jesus appearing to his disciples, which happened in Galilee after he had met with his disciples in Jerusalem.

I'm going fishing

Seven of the disciples were together on the shores of Lake Galilee, Peter and John among them.

"I'm going fishing," said Peter. It was the job he had done before he met Jesus.

The others decided to go with him. But in spite of their years of experience, they didn't catch anything all night. As the sun was rising, they headed for the shore. A man was watching them.

"Young men, haven't you caught anything?" he called.

"Not a thing," they answered.

He said, "Throw your net out on the right side and you will catch some."

They did so, and at once the net was so full of fish they could not pull it in.

Then John looked more carefully. "It is the Lord!" he said to Peter. At that, Peter jumped into the water and swam ashore, leaving the others to bring the boat in. Jesus had a charcoal fire burning, and he asked for some fish to cook.

Three questions

When Jesus met his disciples in Galilee, three times he asked Peter if he loved him.

A third time Jesus said, "Simon son of John, do you love me?"

Peter became sad because Jesus asked him the third time, "Do you love me?" and so he said to him, "Lord, you know everything; you know that I love you!"

John 21:17

Jesus told Peter to take care of all his followers and to be faithful to him until he died. It was as if Peter were being asked to make up for the three times he denied knowing Jesus on the night of the arrest.

Peter jumped out of the boat in order to be the first to shore . . . where Jesus was waiting.

51 Jesus Says Goodbye

When Jesus appeared to his followers he explained to them the meaning of all that had happened. He told them to continue the work he had begun.

"The Messiah must suffer and must rise from death three days later, and in his name the message about repentance and the forgiveness of sins must be preached to all nations, beginning in Jerusalem."

Luke 24:46–47

"Go, then, to all peoples everywhere and make them my disciples: baptize them in the name of the Father, the Son, and the Holy Spirit, and teach them to obey everything I have commanded you."

Matthew 28:19–20

Peter told the crowd of believers that either Joseph or Matthias could take the place of Judas Iscariot.

Look It Up

Jesus says goodbye:
Matthew 28, Luke 24, also Mark 16, John 20, 21, Acts 1

Jesus goes to heaven:
Luke 24, Acts 1, also Mark 16

✝ Baptism

In many churches, people who are new to the Christian faith are welcomed with the ceremony of baptism. As they are dipped in water or splashed with a little water, the words "In the name of the Father, the Son, and the Holy Spirit" are said. These are the same words Jesus told his disciples to use. The person who is being baptized also promises to obey Jesus' teachings.

Some churches baptize newborn babies. In this case, the parents and godparents promise to raise the child to know about Jesus and to live as he taught.

In some churches, a silver shell is used to scoop a little water over the head of someone who is being baptized.

Jesus goes to heaven

Luke tells the most dramatic story of what happened after that.

Jesus led the disciples out of Jerusalem as far as Bethany. There, he raised his hands and blessed them. As he was blessing them, he departed from them and was taken up into heaven.

A cloud hid him from their sight. They still had their eyes fixed on the sky as he went away. Suddenly, there were two men in white standing beside them.

"Why are you looking at the sky?" they asked. "This Jesus, who was taken from you into heaven, will come back in the same way that you saw him go to heaven."

After they had seen Jesus go, the eleven disciples went back to Jerusalem and worshiped God in the Temple there. They often met to pray together, along with the women who had stayed faithful to Jesus. Mary, Jesus' mother, was also part of the group, along with other relatives whom Luke describes as Jesus' brothers.

One day, about a hundred and twenty believers were gathered together. Peter announced that he thought it was right to choose someone to take the place of Judas Iscariot. Two people were suggested—Joseph and Matthias. Then they prayed that God would show them which of the two should be appointed, and they drew lots. Matthias was chosen.

✠ The Ascension

Jesus' going back to heaven is remembered in many Christian churches and known as the Ascension. The festival happens on a Thursday, forty days after Easter.

This is the traditional site of the Ascension, near Jerusalem. A chapel has been built around a footprint-shaped indentation.

Apostles

Jesus' disciples are also called the apostles. The word *apostles* means "ones who are sent." The disciples were being sent out by Jesus to spread the news about Jesus and God's kingdom.

The Acts of the Apostles

Luke's second book, the most important account of what happened to the first followers of Jesus, is in the Bible. It is called the Acts of the Apostles, or sometimes the book of Acts, and it was Luke's sequel to his Gospel.

52  The Holy Spirit

Look It Up

The Holy Spirit:
Acts 2

Gifts of the Spirit:
1 Corinthians 12–14

✠ Speaking in tongues

On the day of Pentecost, the believers found themselves speaking in foreign languages that pilgrims from other parts of the empire understood.

In some churches, "speaking in tongues" is still a regular part of the worship. Nowadays the worshipers who do this usually say that God gives them the ability to speak in languages neither they, nor anyone else, understand, but that inspire both them and others to praise God.

The branch of the present-day church that first brought this practice back into favor is called the Pentecostal church, out of respect for the first Christian Day of Pentecost.

Jesus told his followers not to rush out spreading the message. Instead they were to stay quietly in Jerusalem until they were given power from God, the Holy Spirit.

Ten days after Jesus went back to heaven it was the Jewish feast of Pentecost, the harvest festival. Once again, Jerusalem was busy with pilgrims from all over the world.

Jesus' followers were all together. Suddenly they heard a sound like a strong wind blowing, and something like tongues of fire spread out and touched everyone.

They were transformed with power from God—"filled with the Holy Spirit"—and suddenly they were able to speak other languages. Very soon, a crowd gathered: the pilgrims could hear local people speaking their own language about God and the great things God had done. They were intrigued.

The disciples were in a locked room, afraid to go out.

When the disciples received strength from God's Holy Spirit, they rushed out to tell all Jerusalem about Jesus.

Then Peter stood up and spoke to the crowd. He explained that, in Jesus, everything spoken of in the Jewish Scriptures was coming true and that Jesus was the Messiah.

The people were perplexed. "What shall we do?" they asked.

Peter said to them, "Each one of you must turn away from your sins and be baptized in the name of Jesus Christ, so that your sins will be forgiven; and you will receive God's gift, the Holy Spirit. . . . Save yourselves from the punishment coming on this wicked people!"

Acts 2:38–40

Many of the people were convinced by what Peter said, and three thousand were baptized.

Jesus, by his life and death, had already transformed his small band of followers. His message was about to transform the world.

Gifts of the Spirit

The gifts of the Holy Spirit were not just for Jesus' followers on the Day of Pentecost, claimed one of the first Christians. He wrote a letter to explain:

There are different kinds of spiritual gifts, but the same Spirit gives them. There are different ways of serving, but the same Lord is served. There are different abilities to perform service, but the same God gives ability to all for their particular service. The Spirit's presence is shown in some way in each person for the good of all.

1 Corinthians 12:4–7

He believed that every Christian would have some special God-given ability—something that would contribute to the life of the church.

However, he added that the most important thing for Christians to do was to show unfailing love for one another.

Meanwhile these three remain: faith, hope, and love; and the greatest of these is love.

1 Corinthians 13:13

53 The Believers in Jerusalem

After the Day of Pentecost, the number of people who believed the news about Jesus grew and grew. They treated one another as family, sharing their possessions with one another so that no one was left in need and meeting in each others' homes to share joyful meals. Even the people who did not believe in Jesus were impressed by the way they lived.

Trouble ahead

The religious leaders in Jerusalem were dismayed. After all, it was they who had arranged for Jesus to be put to death. They had not expected his followers to regroup with such enthusiasm and success. They ordered Peter and John to be brought to them and warned them sternly to stop preaching. Peter and John answered them boldly:

"You yourselves judge which is right in God's sight—to obey you or to obey God. For we cannot stop speaking of what we ourselves have seen and heard."

Acts 4:19–20

An angel let Peter and John out of jail.

They were let go with a warning and continued to spread the news more and more. The council of Jewish religious leaders then had them thrown into jail, but—as Luke describes it—in the night an angel opened the gates and let them out. The apostles went to the Temple and continued preaching.

The council had them rearrested as quietly as possible and once again ordered them to stop preaching about Jesus and his resurrection. Again they refused. At this point, many in the council wanted to have them put to death, but one man, named Gamaliel, began to speak.

He reminded them of two notorious men who had been local heroes and had gathered a rabble of followers. But once they had been killed, their followers had scattered. Gamaliel continued:

Look It Up

Miracles and wonders:
Acts 2–4

Deacons:
Acts 6

The believers in Jerusalem:
Acts 2–5

Stephen:
Acts 6–7

Miracles and wonders

Soon after they began preaching, Peter and John performed a spectacular miracle in Jerusalem. They healed a crippled man who for years had sat begging by the Temple. There were many reports of other miracles too. As a result, many people believed the apostles' message and the religious leaders in the council were as perplexed as ever.

✝ Deacons

The apostles chose seven helpers to look after the practical details of organizing the group of believers. The Greek word for *helper* (*diakonos*) has become the word *deacon* in English. Many churches today give this title to people who hold a particular role in the church.

"And so in this case, I tell you, do not take any action against these men. Leave them alone! If what they have planned and done is of human origin, it will disappear, but if it comes from God, you cannot possibly defeat them. You could find yourselves fighting against God!"
Acts 5:38–39

Stephen

Around this time, the apostles found that they were spending more time than seemed sensible organizing the way money was shared among the believers. They wanted to give more time to preaching, so they chose seven helpers to handle the practical details about money. One of these helpers was a man named Stephen, and he was able to work miracles in Jesus' name. He got drawn into an argument about Jesus with some fellow Jews. They were unable to argue with him so they had him dragged before the council.

Once again, Stephen put forward the case for believing in Jesus. He gave a long speech and quoted stories from the Jewish Scriptures to show how, time and again, the people had rejected God's leading.

According to legend, Lawrence was laid on a metal rack and roasted to death for refusing to abandon his faith. It is said that he remained cheerful to the end.

"Was there any prophet that your ancestors did not persecute? They killed God's messengers, who long ago announced the coming of his righteous Servant. And now you have betrayed and murdered him. You are the ones who received God's law, that was handed down by angels—yet you have not obeyed it!"
Acts 7:52–53

In a rage, the council dragged Stephen outside the city. The people involved threw off their cloaks and asked a young man named Saul to watch over them. Then— ignoring the Roman law which insisted that only a Roman official could approve the death penalty—they stoned Stephen to death.

As Stephen met his death, says Luke, he looked up to heaven and saw God's glory and Jesus standing at the right-hand side of God.

✚ Martyrs

When Stephen was put to death for his faith he became Christianity's first martyr. In the following centuries, many Roman Christians were thrown to the lions as entertainment. Over the course of history, many Christians have been martyred for their faith. They are greatly respected by the church for their trust in God as they met their deaths.

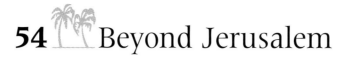

This map shows the places to which some of Jesus' disciples traveled, spreading the message of Christianity as they went.

Peter brought the news about Jesus to a Roman officer in Caesarea—a garrison town on the coast with a splendid Roman amphitheatre.

After Stephen had been put to death, the religious leaders in Jerusalem tried to round up the believers and have them thrown into jail. Saul, who had watched with grim approval as Stephen was stoned, went from house to house trying to find them.

In a way, what they did only helped spread the news. The believers fled to places where they felt they would be safer, and wherever they went they told their news.

Philip

Philip, one of the seven helpers, went to Samaria. Religious Jews looked down on the Samaritans and criticized them for not having a proper understanding of their faith, but Philip was happy to preach to them about Jesus. Many people believed and were baptized. Peter and John came to bless them, and as they laid their hands on them, the new believers were filled with the Holy Spirit.

After that, Philip traveled south, along the road from Jerusalem to Gaza. As he journeyed, he saw an Ethiopian traveling in style. In fact, he was in charge of the treasury of the Queen of Ethiopia. Philip felt led by the Holy Spirit to go and talk to him, and when he got close, he realized that the Ethiopian was reading from the book of Isaiah, part of the Jewish Scriptures. Philip offered to explain the meaning of the passage. He told the Ethiopian that the prophet had foretold the coming of Jesus.

The official was convinced. When he saw a pool by the side of the road, he asked to be baptized at once.

A foreigner—a Gentile—had become a follower of Jesus.

Philip agreed to baptize an Ethiopian who wished to become a Christian.

Peter and Cornelius

Peter, too, traveled to spread the news about Jesus. His miracles caused many to marvel—not least in the town of Joppa when he raised to life a woman named Tabitha. Her widow friends had come to the house to mourn her death. When they realized that Peter had brought her to life, they told everyone they knew!

One day in Joppa, Peter went onto the roof of the house where he was staying to pray quietly. He became hungry, but the meal was not yet ready. In the noonday heat, he had a vision. It was as if a sheet full of animals were being lowered from heaven, and a voice said to him, "Get up, Peter, kill and eat."

Peter refused. The creatures were the ones that were forbidden as food for Jews. Then the voice spoke again: "Do not consider anything unclean that God has declared clean." This happened three times.

At that moment, travelers arrived. They had been sent by a Roman officer named Cornelius, who lived in the garrison town of Caesarea. He was an admirer of the Jewish faith. An angel had visited him and told him to send for Simon Peter.

Little by little Peter began to understand. The vision was God's way of telling him that the barrier between Jews and Gentiles was being broken down. The Jewish laws did not allow him to visit a Gentile, but God wanted him to go and tell Cornelius and his household about Jesus.

Shortly after he had been welcomed into Cornelius's home, he began to preach: "I now realize that God treats everyone on the same basis. Those who worship him and do what is right are acceptable to him no matter what race they belong to."

As the Roman household listened to the account of Jesus' life, death, and resurrection, they were filled with the Holy Spirit. It was like the Day of Pentecost all over again. News of this spread to all the believers, and even those in Jerusalem had to agree that both Jews and Gentiles were welcome in God's kingdom.

Messengers from a Roman officer asked Peter to come and tell the household about Jesus.

The emperor Nero gives the sign for a prisoner to be put to death. It is thought that Nero ordered Peter's crucifixion, and that Peter asked to be crucified upside down as he was less worthy than Jesus.

What happened to the disciples?

Very little is known about what happened to Jesus' disciples after the resurrection.

Peter was married, and probably traveled with his wife to spread the news about Jesus. He went to Rome and, from there, wrote a letter to other Christians. A second letter in the New Testament also bears his name. Peter was probably put to death by the notorious emperor Nero.

John, too, eagerly spread the news, even though his brother James was put to death in Jerusalem. It is thought that he settled in the town of Ephesus with Jesus' mother, Mary. He is traditionally believed to have written John's Gospel. Many believe he also wrote the letters in the New Testament that bear his name. Another tradition says that when he was very old he would urge people to remember one thing above all else: "Little children, love one another."

55 Jesus Appears to Saul

Luke and Paul

The story of Paul is told in Luke's book, the Acts of the Apostles. It appears that at some point Luke becomes one of Paul's traveling companions—as you can tell from this passage, which reads like a travel diary:

We left by ship from Troas and sailed straight across to Samothrace, and the next day to Neapolis. From there we went inland to Philippi, a city of the first district of Macedonia; it is also a Roman colony. . . . We went out of the city to the riverside . . . and talked to the women who gathered there.

Acts 16:11–13

The ruins of Philippi—a town to where Luke and Paul traveled.

Although many of the followers of Jesus had fled Jerusalem after Stephen's death, Saul wanted to hunt them down. He was a devout Jew, and it offended him greatly to think that rumors about Jesus were leading people astray.

He set off, with the approval of the high priest, for Damascus. He had heard that people were preaching about Jesus in the synagogues there.

As he came near the city, a light from the sky flashed around him. Saul fell to the ground. He heard a voice saying, "Saul, Saul, why do you persecute me?"

"Who are you?" Saul asked.

"I am Jesus, whom you persecute," said the voice. "But go into the city, and you will be told what you must do."

Paul was blinded by a bright light on the road to Damascus. Then he heard Jesus speaking.

The men traveling with Saul heard the voice but did not see anyone. Saul found he was suddenly blind and had to be led to Damascus.

At the same time, a Christian in Damascus had a vision from God telling him to go and explain the news about Jesus to Saul.

Saul begins to preach

Saul became an ardent believer and himself began preaching about Jesus in the synagogues. He became so persuasive that some of the Jews in Damascus wanted to kill him. Saul's friends had to smuggle him out of the city—lowering him from the city walls in a basket one dark night.

He escaped to Jerusalem, where the believers were naturally suspicious of him. It was only because one man, Barnabas, believed his story that he was accepted.

All the time, news about Jesus was spreading. A lively group of believers met in a place called Antioch, and Paul and Barnabas spent a year there. Then the believers decided that it was God's will for them to send Paul and Barnabas on a mission to spread the news further.

Saul becomes Paul

As he traveled the empire, Saul became known by the Roman version of his name, Paul. He visited many different places. To stay in touch with the new believers, he wrote letters—teaching and encouraging them. What he wrote was highly respected. His letters were copied to other groups, and several of them are included in the Bible.

Paul finally ran into trouble with the authorities and was arrested. He had the useful status of being a Roman citizen and was able to demand that he be tried by the emperor.

The last years of his life were spent under house arrest in Rome, where he continued to write letters about Jesus.

Throughout, Paul was driven by the unshakeable belief that Jesus had risen from the dead. Jesus' resurrection was a sign of God's power to give new life to all who believed in him. Paul wrote this:

God has made Christ to be our wisdom. By him we are put right with God; we become God's holy people and are set free.

1 Corinthians 1:30

✝ The Church

Very soon, each group of believers was called a church. The word referred to the people, not a building. News about Jesus was often preached in Jewish synagogues or public meeting places. Believers met in one another's homes.

✝ Christians

Luke tells us in Acts that it was at the church in Antioch that those who believed in Jesus were first called Christians. In accepting this name, believers declare their faith that Jesus is God's Messiah, God's Christ (see page 6).

This series of maps shows the three missionary journeys of Paul and his final voyage to Rome.

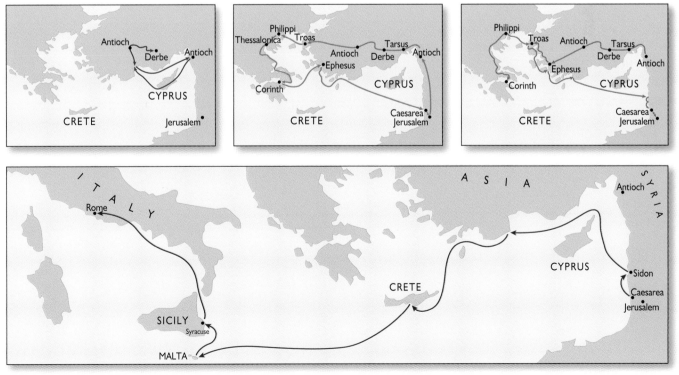

56  A Vision of Jesus

The first Christians believed that one day Jesus would come back. His return would mark the beginning of a whole new world.

Doubt in Thessalonica

As time passed and some believers died, people began to lose confidence. Some Christians in Thessalonica had been so sure that Jesus would return they had given up work. Paul told them they must get on with living wisely, for only God knew when the end would come.

Hope through persecution

Meanwhile, life was often difficult for people who declared themselves Christians. At the end of the first century, the emperor Domitian began a new wave of persecution. He sent a Christian named John to the labor camps on the prison island of Patmos for spreading the news about Jesus.

While he was there, John had a vision of Jesus:

I saw . . . what looked like a human being, wearing a robe that reached to his feet, and a gold band around his chest. His hair was white as wool, or as snow, and his eyes blazed like fire; his feet shone like brass that has been refined and polished, and his voice sounded like a roaring waterfall. He held seven stars in his right hand, and a sharp two-edged sword came out of his mouth. His face was as bright as the midday sun.

Revelation 1:12–16

Look It Up

Waiting for Jesus:
1 Thessalonians 5, 2 Thessalonians 3

Hope through persecution:
Revelation 1, 22

Heaven:
John 14, Revelation 21, 22

Saints
Revelation 13

Waiting for Jesus

Some Christians expected Jesus to return very soon. Paul wrote to the Christians in Thessalonica with advice about how to live their lives as they waited.

We must wear faith and love as a breastplate, and our hope of salvation as a helmet.

1 Thessalonians 5:8

We urge you, our friends, to warn the idle, encourage the timid, help the weak, be patient with everyone. See that no one pays back wrong for wrong, but at all times make it your aim to do good to one another and to all people.

Be joyful always, pray at all times, be thankful in all circumstances.

1 Thessalonians 5:14–18

You, friends, must not become tired of doing good.

2 Thessalonians 3:13

A Christian named John wrote a book about an amazing vision. In the vision he saw Jesus holding seven stars. Then Jesus explained these were seven churches to whom he must write words of warning and encouragement.

✜ Heaven

The words of Revelation have inspired a traditional Christian view of heaven.

It is a city of gold enclosed within a high wall. Each of the twelve gates is made from pearl. The river of the water of life flows through the city, and on each side of the river stands the tree of life. There is no sun, moon, or stars, but only the light of God and Jesus.

Christians believe they will go to heaven because of these words of Jesus:

"Do not be worried and upset. . . . Believe in God and believe also in me. There are many rooms in my Father's house, and I am going to prepare a place for you. . . . I will come back and take you to myself, so that you will be where I am."

John 14:1–3

The angel shows John the heavenly city.

A vision of heaven

John's book then describes heaven itself. He saw people and angels and many strange beasts. He saw a lamb upon a throne—a symbol of Jesus, who was killed like a sacrificial lamb.

The puzzling events described the conflict of good and evil. Many people believed they were a message of encouragement, that the Roman empire would not destroy the Christian faith.

In the end, John had a vision of a new heaven and a new earth. Death and grief were defeated, and those who loved God worshiped God joyfully. Finally, John gave a message from Jesus:

"Listen!" says Jesus. "I am coming soon! I will bring my rewards with me, to give to each one according to what he has done. I am the first and the last, the beginning and the end.

"Happy are those who wash their robes clean and so have the right to eat the fruit from the tree of life and to go through the gates into the city. . . . I, Jesus, have sent my angel to announce these things to you in the churches. I am descended from the family of David; I am the bright morning star."

John's book, Revelation, is the last book of the Bible, and concludes:

So be it. Come, Lord Jesus!
May the grace of the Lord Jesus be with everyone.

Revelation 22:12–16, 20–21

✜ Saints

In some older translations of the Bible, the people who believe in Jesus are referred to as saints. The word means that they are truly God's people.

In some church traditions the title of Saint is given to people whose lives have been a shining example of faith and who have been linked to proven miracles.

One of Christianity's best-loved saints is Francis of Assisi, who faithfully modeled his life of poverty and humility on the words of Jesus.

57 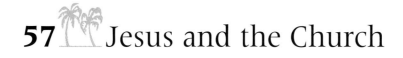 Jesus and the Church

Look It Up

What to believe:
Genesis 1, Psalm 33, John 3, Matthew 26, Mark 14, Luke 22, Acts 10, I Corinthians 15

✠ Ichthus

This word *icthus* is the Greek word for fish, and the fish was a secret symbol of the Christians persecuted under Roman rule. The letters of the word reminded Christians of Jesus and their belief in him.

IESOUS	Jesus
CHRISTOS	Christ
THEOU	of God
HUIOS	son
SOTER	savior

Chi-Rho

The symbol that Constantine adopted was the Chi-Rho—the names of two letters in the Greek alphabet and the first two letters of the word *Christ.* The Chi-Rho is an emblem often seen in churches.

As the years went by, the people who had actually known Jesus grew old and eventually died. However, the number of Christians continued to grow, even though the Roman rulers were suspicious of them and frequently persecuted them.

Jesus and the emperor

In the year 312, the Roman emperor, Constantine, was preparing for battle. The day before his armies were due to fight, he saw a vision in the sky—the cross symbol that Christians used. Around it were the Latin words, *In hoc signo vinces*—by this sign, you shall conquer.

That night, Constantine had a dream in which Jesus appeared to him and told him he must make the symbol his own. The following day Constantine won the battle. He made Christianity the official religion of his empire. Although it seems highly improbable that Jesus would ever have forced people to become his followers, the ruling did allow the faith to be spread more easily.

East and west

From very early times, there had been important churches in two cities: Rome, in the very heart of the Roman empire, and Constantinople, further to the east. Over the years, the two churches developed different ways of worship, and in the eleventh century they split. The church in the west became known as the Roman Catholic church, and the one in the east, the Eastern Orthodox. *Catholic* is simply a word for "universal" and *orthodox* comes from the Greek words *orthos* and *doxa*, meaning "right belief" or "true doctrine."

Catholics and Protestants

Throughout the Middle Ages, the Roman Catholic church held a great deal of wealth and power in Europe. There were many sincere Christians who tried to live as Jesus taught, but the institution appeared to have grown corrupt. In the sixteenth century, a Roman Catholic monk named Martin Luther nailed up a list of questions he wanted to discuss with the authorities. They were about the differences between what the church did and what the Bible said. This led to a bitter fight, and Luther was rejected by the church in 1521.

This was a turning point for a new movement among Christians who wanted to read the Bible for themselves and discover its teaching. They became known as Protestants. Many different groups of Protestants emerged—including the Baptists and the Presbyterians.

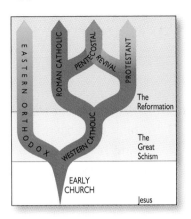

This diagram shows the major branches of the Christian church and how they developed.

Revival and the Pentecostals

In 1906, members of a Protestant church in Los Angeles began having the same kinds of experiences as the disciples did on the Day of Pentecost—they felt filled with the Holy Spirit and spoke in tongues. Some found they were able to heal people "in the name of Jesus." Soon Pentecostal groups were springing up everywhere. The Pentecostal movement has since influenced many other parts of the church.

One church, one faith, one Lord

Since Jesus walked this earth, around two thousand years ago, belief in him has spread around the world. Christians from every type of church have witnessed to the importance of their faith and done many good things to increase peace and justice. Sadly, Christians have often argued among themselves about such things as the right way to organize a church and which beliefs are the most important. However, all Christians agree that Jesus is at the heart of the faith: that his teaching and example are for believers to follow, and that his death and resurrection open the way for all people to become God's people.

✛ What to believe

From the beginning, Christians have debated exactly what to believe about their faith. For this reason, there have been many attempts to put together a statement of belief, or creed. This one, known as the Apostles' Creed, dates from the second century. Still said by many Christians around the world, it tries to draw together a summary of what is important about Jesus, using the testimony of his first followers.

*I believe in God the Father
   almighty,
creator of heaven and earth.*

*I believe in Jesus Christ,
   his only Son, our Lord,
who was conceived by the
   Holy Spirit,
born of the Virgin Mary,
suffered under Pontius Pilate,
was crucified, died and
   was buried;
he descended to the dead.
On the third day he rose again;
he ascended into heaven,
he is seated at the right hand
   of the Father,
and he will come to judge
   the living and the dead.*

*I believe in the Holy Spirit,
the holy catholic Church,
the communion of saints,
the forgiveness of sins,
the resurrection of the body,
and the life everlasting.
Amen.*

Common Worship

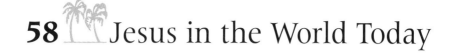

Jesus of Nazareth lived and died two thousand years ago. He was born to an ordinary working family in a backwater of the Roman empire. Today, his name is better known around the world than that of any of the emperors.

✝ Christian culture

From early times, Christianity had a major influence in Europe, and this influence spread to places where European explorers opened the way for emigrants to settle. In places such as these, there is evidence of Christian culture even among the many people who say they are not religious. Christmas, for example, is a major festival, and the story of Jesus' birth is told and retold among all the glitter and tinsel of a major spending extravaganza. People still choose churches as places for weddings, and many turn to the church to provide hope and comfort when they face bereavement.

A growing church

One in three people in the world declare themselves to be Christians. In some countries, including the ones where Christianity has been the main religion for hundreds of years, it is often the case that fewer and fewer people attend a Christian church. However, in many other parts of the world, the number of believers is growing rapidly and church congregations are larger than ever before. Christianity seems to have particular appeal wherever there is poverty and injustice.

Peace and justice

Jesus' life and teaching inspire millions to play their part in working for peace and justice. There are many Christian organizations dedicated to relieving poverty, helping in disaster zones, and showing solidarity with those who are oppressed. There are also many Christians in secular organizations that have these aims. Christians—

Jesus welcomed children to be part of God's kingdom. This little girl is saying prayers to him.

Jesus' death on a cross is at the heart of the Christian faith. In the Church of Melanesia in Tagabe, on the outskirts of Port Vila, Vanuatu, a symbolic cross is carried into the church meeting. This type of ceremony takes place in many churches around the world.

who believe in Jesus' resurrection from a criminal's death—trust in God's power to overcome everything that is evil and destructive, and to give eternal life.

Faith and worship

All over the world and in the many branches of the Christian church, believers meet to learn together, worship together, and pray together. Sometimes they gather in glittering cathedrals. Sometimes they gather among the rubbish heaps of shanty towns. Whatever their situation, they learn from Jesus' teaching that they must not be concerned with material possessions but with the things that lead to eternal life in God's kingdom.

Witnesses to Jesus

Christians take very seriously the last words of Jesus to his disciples. They are enthusiastic for their faith and eager to share it with others, by the things they say and the things they do. They often speak of the sense of peace and purpose that comes from their faith and their hope of eternal life.

Jesus declared himself to be "the light of the world." At this Easter church gathering, children outside the Church of the Annunciation, Tirana, Albania, hold candles to remind themselves of the hope that their faith gives them.

Christians declare that their faith brings them joy. Their worship often includes happy and joyful singing—as shown by this choir from Ethiopia, at the Trinity Cathedral in Addis Ababa.

Holy liturgy in an Orthodox Women's Monastery close to Moscow, Russia. Orthodox Christian worship is full of ceremony that emphasizes the mystery of faith and the holiness of God.

A world with many faiths

Jesus is recorded as saying that he alone was the way to God, and Christians declare that their faith is unique. Nevertheless, in today's world, where communication and travel bring people from different cultures together, there is much respect and understanding between the faiths.

Christianity is rooted in the Jewish faith—Jesus himself was a Jew and had the highest regard for the Scriptures of his people, as Christians do today. The greatest prophet of Islam, Muhammad, taught and preached from a background that included Jewish and Christian influences. Indeed, Jesus himself is regarded as a prophet in Islam, and known in that faith as Isa.

The major Eastern faiths— Hinduism, Buddhism, and Sikhism—all have some common ground with Christianity. This includes a shared commitment to living in a way that is pure and good and just.

Index

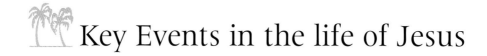

Key Events in the life of Jesus

	Matthew	Mark	Luke	John
Announcement of the birth of John the Baptist			1:5–23	
Announcement of the birth of Jesus	1:18–24		1:26–38	
Jesus' mother, Mary, visits Elizabeth			1:39–56	
Birth of John the Baptist			1:57–79	
Birth of Jesus	1:25		2:1–39	
Visit of the shepherds			2:8–20	
Visit of the wise men	2:1–12			
Escape to Egypt and return to Nazareth	2:13–23			
The boy Jesus in the Temple			2:41–50	
John the Baptist's message	3:1–12	1:1–8	3:1–18	1:19–28
Jesus' baptism	3:13–17	1:9–11	3:21–22	1:29–34
Jesus' temptation	4:1–11	1:12–13	4:1–13	
Meeting with Nicodemus				3:1–21
Meeting with the woman from Samaria				4:1–42
Jesus is rejected in Nazareth			4:16–30	
Call of the disciples Andrew, Simon, James and John	4:18–22	1:16–20	5:1–11	
Call of Matthew (Levi)	9:9–13	2:13–17	5:27–32	
Jesus chooses 12 disciples	10:2–4	3:13–19	6:12–16	
The Sermon on the Mount	5:1–7:28		6:20–49	
Death of John the Baptist	14:1–12	6:14–29	9:7–9	
Peter acknowledges Jesus as the Christ	16:13–20	8:27–30	9:18–21	
Jesus foretells his death	16:21–28	8:31–9:1	9:22–27	
The transfiguration of Jesus	17:1–13	9:2–13	9:28–36	
Jesus with Martha and Mary			10:38–42	
Jesus meets Zachaeus in Jericho			19:1–10	
Jesus and Lazarus				11:1–44
Palm Sunday	21:1–11	11:1–11	19:28–44	12:12–16
Judas' betrayal and rulers' plots	26:1–5, 14–16	14;1–2, 10–11	20:19, 22:1–6	11:45–57
The Passover meal/Last Supper	26:17–29	14:12–25	22:7–38	13:1–20
Jesus in Gethsemane	26:36–46	14:32–42	22:39–46	
Jesus is arrested	26:47–56	14:43–52	22:47–53	18:2–12
Jesus on trial	26:57–27:1	14:53–15:1	22:54–71	18:13–24
Peter denies Jesus	26:69–75	14:66–71	22:54–62	18:15, 25–27
Jesus and Pilate	27:2–30	15:1–19	23:1–25	18:28–19:15
Jesus is crucified and buried	27:31–66	15:20–47	23:26–56	19:16–42
Resurrection and resurrection appearances	28:1–15	16:1–8, 9–14	24:1–49	20:1–21:23
Jesus goes into heaven		16:19–20	24:50–53	

The Parables of Jesus

Parables included in this book are in bold. There are no parables in John's Gospel.

	Matthew	Mark	Luke
The lamp under a bowl	5:14–16	4:21–22	8:16, 11:33
Houses built on rock and sand	7:24–27	6:47–49	
New cloth sewn on an old garment	9:16	2:21	5:36
New wine poured in old wineskins	9:17	2:22	5:37–38
The sower and the different soils	13:3–9, 18–23	4:3–8, 13–20	8:5–8, 11–15
The mustard seed	13:31–32	4:30–32	13:18–19
The wheat and the weeds	13:24–30, 36–43		
The yeast in the dough	13:33		13:20–21
Hidden treasure	13:44		
The priceless pearl	13:45–46		
The net	13:47–50		
The lost sheep	18:12–14		15:4–7
The unforgiving servant	18:23–25		
The workers in the vineyard	20:1–16		
The two sons	21:28–32		
The tenants in the vineyard	21:33–44	12:1–9	20:9–16
The great feast	22:2–14		14:16–24
The fig tree	24:32–33	13:28–29	21:29–31
Ten young women	25:1–13		
The talents (Matthew); pounds (Luke)	25:14–30		19:12–27
The sheep and the goats	25:31–46		
Seed-time to harvest		4:26–29	
The creditor and the debtors			7:41–50
The good Samaritan			10:30–37
The friend in need			11:5–10
The rich fool			12:16–21
The alert servants			12:35–40
The faithful steward			12:42–48
The fig tree without figs			13:6–9
The places of honour at the feast			14:7–14
The great banquet and the reluctant guests			14:16–24
Counting the cost			14:28–33
The lost coin			15:8–10
The lost son			15:11–32
The dishonest steward			16:1–8
The rich man and Lazarus			16:19–31
The master and the servant			17:7–10
The persistent widow and the unrighteous judge			18:2–8
The Pharisee and the tax collector			18:10–14

The miracles of Jesus

	Matthew	Mark	Luke	John
Miracles of Healing				
Leper	8:2–4	1:40–44	5:12–14	
Centurion's servant	8:5–13		7:1–10	
Simon Peter's mother-in-law	8:14–15	1:30–-31	4:38–39	
Possessed man	8:28–34	5:1–15	8:27–35	
Paralysed man	9:2–7	2:3–12	5:18–25	
Woman with a haemorrhage	9:20–22	5:25–34	8:43–48	
Two blind men	9:27–31			
Man who was dumb and 'possessed'	9:32–33			
Man with a paralysed hand	12:10–13	3:1–5	6:6–10	
Man who was dumb, blind and 'possessed'	12:22			
Canaanite woman's daughter	15:21–28	7:24–30		
Boy with epilepsy	17:14–18	9:17–29	9:38–43	
Bartimaeus and another blind man	20:29–34	10:46–52	18:35–43	
Deaf and dumb man		7:31–37		
Man who was 'possessed'		1:23–26	4:33–35	
Blind man at Bethsaida		8:22–26		
Woman who was bent double			13:11–13	
Man with dropsy			14:1–4	
Ten lepers			17:11–19	
High priest's servant's ear			22:50–51	
Official's son at Capernaum				4:46–53
Sick man, pool of Bethsaida				5:1–9
Man born blind				9
Power over natural forces				
Calming of the storm on the lake	8:23–27	4:37–41	8:22–25	
Walking on the water	14:25–31	6:48–51		6:19–21
Feeding 5,000 people	14:15–21	6:35–44	9:12–17	6:5–13
Feeding 4,000 people	15:32–38	8:1–9		
Coin in the fish's mouth	17:24–27			
Fig-tree withered	21:18–22	11:12–14, 20–26		
Catch of fish			5:1–11	
Water turned into wine				2:1–11
Another catch of fish			21:1–11	
Bringing the dead back to life				
Jairus's daughter	9:18–19, 23–25	5:22–24, 38–43	8:41–42, 49–56	
Widow's son at Nain		7:11–15		
Lazarus				11:1–44